Torah Encounters

NUMBERS

The Torah Encounters series presents selections from both ancient and contemporary Torah commentaries. Modern readers, with or without previous Torah study, will find themselves drawn into a discussion of the deeper meaning of each week's portion. The series is based on the renowned Torah Sparks guides created by Rabbi Daniel Pressman for the United Synagogue of Conservative Judiasm and used in synagogues throughout North and South America.

NUMBERS

Torah Encounters

Rabbi Daniel Pressman

United Synagogue of Conservative Judaism
ROWMAN & LITTLEFIELD
Lanham | Boulder | New York | London

The publication of Torah Encounters was made possible by a generous gift from Ann and Rick Tavan.

Published in cooperation with United Synagogue of Conservative Judaism.

Published by Rowman & Littlefield
An imprint of The Rowman & Littlefield Publishing Group, Inc.
4501 Forbes Boulevard, Suite 200, Lanham, Maryland 20706
www.rowman.com

British Library Cataloguing in Publication Information Available

Library of Congress Cataloging-in-Publication Data Available

Paper: 978-1-5381-7416-6
eBook: 978-1-5381-7417-3

Design and typography by Barry Nostradamus Sher.

Contents

Introduction

Once language is recognized as an aspect of infinite divine wisdom, it cannot have finite meanings. In the same way that no one can ever know the "real" meaning of yehi or from the divine point of view — one can only view the earthly result of the utterance — so one cannot glean the real, finite semantic message of any word of God. It is impossible therefore to present the "true" meaning of any biblical verse. One can only search further and further, digging deeper into the infinite layers of divine wisdom, never reaching the end. Exegesis is an infinite process, and no new discovery negates the previous ones. Different, or even contradictory interpretations have equal validity, because the laws of exclusion have no relevance within divine wisdom. (Joseph Dan, The Heart and the Fountain: An Anthology of Jewish Mystical Experiences.)

"Torah" is a word of great scope and power. Jewish tradition abounds in similes to try to describe its essence, including light, fire, fine wine, and precious oil.

Jewish prayer thanks God for Torah as a gift of eternal love: "With eternal love have you loved your people, the House of Israel. Torah and mitzvot, laws and judgments have you taught. Therefore, Lord our God, when we lie down and when we rise up, we will ponder Your laws."[1]

Torah is first and fundamentally the Five Books of Moses, the holy scroll enshrined in the Ark. Jews read Torah every Shabbat, Monday, and Thursday, as well as all the major holidays, "for they [the Torah and Mitzvot] are our life and length of days." Every time we unfurl the scroll, the verses written by the scribe with such scrupulous care open for us a world of meaning.

We read those words with a special consciousness: that Torah is more than the Five Books. It is midrash of law and story — the Rabbinic commentary on every verse, word, and letter. It is the Talmudic discussion and debate and all the commentaries. It is Biblical interpretation from every generation, and even commentaries on commentaries. It is codes of law with, yes, commentaries of their own.

Torah, as both book and process, is the taproot that penetrates to the heart of Jewish meaning, under-

1. From the prayer, *Ahavat Olam.*

standing, and expression. Torah study is how we mine not just meaning from the text, but our awareness of God's will. As a rabbi, it has been my privilege and challenge every week to encounter the Parashah, and hear its message. The infinitely rich spiritual spring of Torah and commentary has never failed me. "Turn it and turn it again, for it holds everything."

For most of my career, I have engaged in interactive study of the weekly Parashah with my congregation, rather than via a monologue. This opens up the encounter with Torah to the insights and wisdom of the worshipping community — and many surprises!

In 1991 I was approached by the United Synagogue of Conservative Judaism to pioneer a new project: *Nitzotzot Torah,* Torah Sparks. The original audience was the 200 or so "small and isolated congregations," many without a rabbi. The Torah Sparks would provide commentary and discussion questions. I am grateful to my friend and teacher Rabbi Jack Riemer for suggesting my name. Rabbi David Blumenfeld of the United Synagogue was the editor, and provided help, encouragement, and his own extensive knowledge of Torah.

During the six years that I produced the Torah Sparks, many congregations ordered them, and I was pleased on several occasions, when visiting other synagogues, to find that they were being put to good use. The Torah Sparks continue, from other hands, to this day.

The discussion questions were originally designed for group study. I have modified many of them to work better for individual contemplation, but I trust that they will also work in a group setting.

Every darshan has a favorite commentary, a place to use as a jumping-off point. I have favored Rashi, the *Torah Temimah,* and two wonderful books by Zelig Pliskin: *Love Your Neighbor* and *Growth Through Torah.* Rabbi Pliskin always seeks out the *mussar haskel,* the practical ethical application of a verse, and I have learned much from him.

I want to thank the United Synagogue, Rabbi Riemer, and Rabbi Blumenfeld for giving me the opportunity to develop these studies. I thank my father, Rabbi Jacob Pressman, a master darshan, who taught me always to ask, "What do you want them to do?" My mother, Marjorie Pressman, has been an inspiring example of Jewish leadership. My late wife Beverly tolerated my tendency to complete the original Torah Sparks too close to deadline, and the consequent difficult behavior on my part. I thank her for her love, support, and understanding. Thanks also to my children, Aliza, Benjamin, and Rebecca, for putting up with the burden of being a rabbi's kids. They have grown into fine adults with good values, and I cherish them.

I thank my first congregation, Congregation Ner Tamid of South Bay, in Palos Verdes, California, for tolerating my learning curve as I made the transition from straight d'rashah to interactive discussion. I recently retired after 33 wonderful years at Congregation Beth David in Saratoga, California. My congregants participated enthusiastically and thoughtfully in Shabbat morning Torah discussions and encouraged me in my studies, including four sabbaticals.

In 2003, I was fortunate to be a Merrill Fellow at the Harvard Divinity School, during which time I finished the bulk of this manuscript. I thank Dr. Dudley Rose of the Divinity School and Charles Merrill, who sponsored the fellowship.

Thanks also go to Congregation Beth David, and the donors, who made this publication possible, and to Dorrie Berkowitz, who edited with a fine hand, a sharp eye, and good humor.

Finally, and happily, thank you to Helen Tieger, my fiancé, for her love and encouragement, and for adding so much joy to my life.

For forty years, I have sat down with the weekly Torah portion to find in it, first of all, that which speaks to me, and then share that wisdom and inspiration. The Torah has been an unfailing wellspring that has nourished my soul and, I hope, touched others as well. A number of years ago I read a wonderful poem that expresses more eloquently than I ever could the beauties and joys of Torah study:

Torah
Barbara D. Holender

You shall love Adonai your God with all your mind, with all your strength, with all your being. Set these words, which I command you this day, upon your heart.
Even when you hold it in your arms,
you have not grasped it.
Wrapped and turned in upon itself
the scroll says, Not yet.

Even when you take them into your eyes,
you have not seen them; elegant
in their crowns the letters stand aloof.

Even when you taste them in your mouth
and roll them on your tongue
or bite the sharp unyielding strokes
they say, Not yet.

And when the sounds pour from your throat
and reach deep into your lungs for breath,
even then the words say, Not quite.

But when your heart knows its own hunger
and your mind is seized and shaken,
and in the narrow space between the lines
your soul builds its nest,

Now, says Torah, now
you begin to understand.

HOW TO USE THIS BOOK

There are many books of comments, essays, and d'rashot on the weekly Parashah. *Torah Encounters* is a little different, because it encourages a personal encounter with the Torah and a large variety of commentaries. Each unit has a title, a theme, and a point, but it ends with open-ended questions for thought, discussion, and hopefully, guidance on how to live a Jewish life. In rereading the book,

I found certain themes recur: the challenges of leadership; the tension between Jewish values and aspects of contemporary culture, in particular the hyper-individualism of our times; ethics; and the need for kindness and compassion. There is also a good deal of theological reflection. Inevitably, these represent my interests and what touched me in my preparation.

So interact with these texts, either by yourself, or preferably in conversation with others. This is not a book to be read, but studied and discussed. Decades ago, in middle school, I learned a way of studying: SQ3R — survey, question, read, recite, and review. For this book I'd suggest: SQ2DA — survey, question, discuss, debate, and apply. The last is the point: Torah study is ultimately not an abstract intellectual exercise — it is a guide to living. As it says in Midrash Genesis Rabbah, "The Torah was given to purify humankind." That is why every morning (Ahavah Rabbah) and evening (Ahavat Olam) we give thanks for God's gift of love, the Torah. I believe that my encounters with these texts have helped me to be a better person than I would have been otherwise — I wish the same for you.

TRANSLITERATION . . . .

. . . . is always a challenge — a tangled thicket of approximation and inconsistency, not to mention a challenge for the editor! By and large in this book, when quoting others, I have left their transliteration scheme alone. My system follows that of the Humash Etz Hayim — with a bit of simplification. Here it is.

Representation	Hebrew Letter	Pronunciation
· [dot]		[break]
a	א or ע	**a**rm
h	ה	**h**oly (or, at end of word, silent)
ḥ	ח	as Johan Sebastian Ba**ch**
i		gr**i**n or pol**i**ce
kh	כ ך	like Scottish "lo**ch**"
o	וֹ	h**o**me
tz	צ ץ	bli**tz**
u	וּ	pl**u**me
'		like Australian "g'day"
ai		Th**ai**land
ei		**ei**ght
oi	וֹי	c**oi**n
ui	וּי	ch**ewy**

2. 44:1

Numbers

The Hebrew name of the book — B'midbar — comes from the first important word and means "in the wilderness," an appropriate name since the wilderness wanderings are the focus of the book. The English name — Numbers —comes from the Latin word numeri and the Greek word arithmoi. Both are probably derived from the Hebrew title in the Mishnah, ḥomesh ha-p'kudim, "the fifth [of the Torah] of the numbered," a reference to the censuses at the beginning and toward the end of the book. The Israeli Bible scholar Shemaryahu Talmon refers to this book as "the Book of Israel's failings," since so much of its narrative tells of the Israelites' complaining and backsliding.

Parshat B'midbar

Num. 1:1–4:20

1. (1:1–16) God orders Moses and Aaron to take a census of the male Israelites of military age, 20 years and older. This is done so that Israel will be able to organize for self-defense during the period of wilderness wandering.
2. (1:17–43) Moses and Aaron and their designated assistants from each tribe take the census. The resulting totals are listed.
3. (1:44–47) The grand total, except for the Levites, is 603,550.
4. (1:48–54) The special tasks of the Levites: taking care of the Tabernacle.
5. (2:1–31) The organization and order of the Israelite camp.
6. (2:32–34) The total enrollment of the Israelites, except for the Levites: 603,550.
7. (3:1–13) The special enrollment of the Levites, their tasks, and the story of how they received their special role in place of the first-born sons.
8. (3:14–39) The enrollment of the Levites from the age of one month and up, according to their respective clans.
9. (3:40–51) The census of the first-born males and the substitution of the Levites for them.
10. (4:1–20) A second census of the Levites between the ages of 30 and 50, this time in order to determine the number needed for their tasks during the period of wilderness wandering. The census of the Kohatites and their appointment to the special task of carrying the holy vessels of the Tabernacle.

QUALITIES TO CULTIVATE

On the first day of the second month, in the second year following the exodus from the land of Egypt, the Lord spoke to Moses in the wilderness of Sinai, in the Tent of Meeting . . . (Num. 1:1)

A. Why *in the wilderness of Sinai?* Our sages have inferred from this that the Torah was given to the accompaniment of three things: fire, water, and wilderness. "Fire," whence was this derived? From the text, *Now Mount Sinai was all in smoke, for the Lord had come down upon it in fire* (Exod. 19:18). And "water," whence is this derived? For it is said, *The heavens dripped, yea the clouds dripped water* (Judg. 5:4).[1] And "Wilderness," whence is this derived? From the text, *the Lord spoke to Moses in the wilderness of Sinai.* (*Midrash Numbers Rabbah* 1:7)

B. These three things symbolize to the Jew how to merit the acquisition of the Torah. Fire: The flame of God, fervor and enthusiasm that burns in the heart of Israel who yearn for their Father in heaven. Water: Coolness and moderation, composure and clarity of thought to consider the importance of the Torah in the correct spirit and with proper insight. Wilderness: Relinquishing all the pleasures and desires of the world that prevent a person from achieving perfection. (Shem MiSh'muel)

We usually think of Judaism as focused on behavior through its elaborate system of law, but there is also an aspect of Jewish thought that concentrates on middot, or character traits. Here we see how this approach takes the imagery of one midrash and learns from it the traits needed to learn, know, and live Torah properly. The role of the "wilderness" is clear: If you get too caught up in the pursuit of pleasure and material gain, you leave yourself no time for Torah study and spiritual growth. But what about the antitheses of fire and water? Why does passion (fire) need to be balanced by clear thinking (water)? Is our Judaism sometimes too cerebral and not passionate enough? On the other hand, what are the dangers of uncontrolled passion?

ON THE THEME OF WILDERNESS: SABBATICALS FOR ALL

A. A people that is in formation must establish and organize itself in every area of its life. First of all it must find the answer to the essential question, For what purpose does it exist? The answer to this was given to the people of Israel at the Giving of the Torah. The people of Israel exist as a nation who keep the Torah and spread it among the nations. . . . The Torah was specifically given in the desert and before the entry into the land, while the people as a whole (and also every individual in particular) were not preoccupied with material concerns and labor, with earning a living, with conducting a state or with warfare, and they were free to receive the Torah and learn it. (Avraham Shtahl, *Shabbat B'Shabbato*)

The last sentence proposes a challenging idea: that in order to fulfill our mission as Jews, we need to be knowledgeable, and in order to do that, we must reserve significant blocks of time for study, for mastering the "operating manual." In Talmudic and post-Talmudic times there was an institution of Yarḥei Kallah — study months — during Elul and Adar. Large numbers of people would assemble to study Torah, some all day, some just in the evening. Many retired people

1. The full context (Judg. 5:4–5): *O Lord, when You came forth from Seir, Advanced from the country of Edom, The earth trembled; The heavens dripped, Yea, the clouds dripped water, The mountains quaked — Before the Lord, Him of Sinai, Before the Lord, God of Israel.* This links God's manifestation at Sinai with water.

today are taking advantage of the proliferation of opportunities for Jewish study. How can the rest of us make the opportunity for undistracted time for Torah study? One possibility is the sabbatical. In her useful book Time Off from Work, Lisa Angowsky Rogak debunks the "Top 5 Myths About Sabbaticals:" 1) You won't come back. 2) Taking time off is the equivalent of a demotion. 3) You'll get lazy. 4) It will set your career back. Maybe, but it also shows initiative and planning ability, especially if your resumé includes what you did and learned. 5) You can't afford it. It does require planning! Many companies are now offering sabbaticals of two to three months. Take a few minutes to consider (or maybe it's more like fantasize) how you could take a sabbatical and what Jewish study you might want to do while on sabbatical. If that doesn't seem feasible, how else could you create protected time for Jewish study?

GENEROSITY COUNTS

Take a census of the whole Israelite community by the clans of their ancestral houses, listing the names, every male, head by head. (Num. 1:2)

A. *Head by head* — i.e., by means of shekels, "a half a shekel a head."[2] (Rashi)

B. Where does Rashi get this from? Our portion doesn't mention that the census is to be done by means of shekels! Rather, when it says take a census [literally: "lift up the heads of the whole Israelite community"], it means that they were counted by means of shekels, for it is impossible for a person be uplifted and achieve spiritual elevation except by means of personal giving and generosity.

There is a custom that when friends dine together at a mitzvah celebration, the honor of leading the Birkat Hamazon is sold off to the one who makes the biggest pledge to tzedakah. By rights, shouldn't this honor go to a Cohen, if one is present, or the greatest in Torah learning or piety among the diners? Rather, this follows what the Sages said (Talmud Sotah 38b): "We give the cup of blessing [the honor of leading the Birkat Hamazon] only to one who is of a generous disposition [literally, "one with a good eye"], as it is said (Prov. 22:9), *The generous one shall be blessed, for he gives of his bread to the poor* — read not *y'vorakh* [shall be blessed] but *y'varekh* [shall say the blessing]." We find that the most generous person among the diners should lead the blessing. Since no one knows the thoughts of another, to discern who is the most generous among the diners, that is why the mitzvah is sold. The one who pledges the most proves that he is the most generous, and is the appropriate person to lead the blessing. *(Min Hatorah)*

There are many ideas in this comment. Among them are:

a) Unless a person is generous, he or she cannot really achieve spiritual elevation.

b) People who are generous deserve public honor.

c) The proof of generosity is in the giving, not in the thought.

---

2. Rashi bases this on Exodus 30:13: *This is what everyone who is entered in the records shall pay: a half-shekel by the sanctuary weight.* Rashi maintains that this is the method to be used in the census mentioned here.

Do you agree with these assertions? How about the specific example: auctioning off an honor? What about the person who gives with great generosity for his or her limited means? Is it fair for him/her to be "outbid" by someone else who gives a larger absolute sum, but one that is relatively small for his/her means? How would we apply this to the once common practice of auctioning off the High Holy Day honors during services?

WHAT IT MEANS TO COUNT

***Take a census of the whole Israelite community by the clans of its ancestral houses, listing the names, every male, by a head count. You and Aaron shall record them by their groups, from the age of twenty years, all those in Israel who are able to bear arms.** (Num. 1:2–3)*

A. Because they were now going to move towards the Land of Israel, and twenty-year-olds are eligible to fight in the army . . . therefore God commanded that they be counted. (Rashbam)

B. God ordered Moses to count them in a manner that would give honor and importance to each and every one of them. You should not say to the head of the family, "How many are there in your family? How many children have you?" But rather all of them should pass before you in awe and with the honor due to them, and you should count them. That is what it meant when it states, *listing the names . . . by a head count.* (Ramban)

C. [The words *s'u et rosh,* translated as "Take a census," literally mean "lift up the head."] Here we see the importance of the people of Israel: every one is a head, an important personality. Therefore, out of noblesse oblige, every Jew must have an extra feeling of responsibility for all his deeds, for he can be a decisive influence for good or for bad. (Rabbi Isaiah Horowitz)

Rashbam gives the p'shat, the contextual meaning of the text. The other two commentators give a d'rash, an interpretation. Ramban learns from the Torah's wording how one should and should not conduct a census. What's the point here? What danger is Ramban trying to avoid? According to Hurvitz, what does the census teach us about our moral obligations? For both: What does it mean to count? ("To count" can mean: 1) to ascertain the whole number of units in a group; 2) to esteem; 3) to take into account; 4) to possess value.) What are the implications for how we organize and participate in Jewish life? How might we apply Rabbi Hurvitz's teaching to the ongoing conflict in Israel about military service for ultra-Orthodox men?

RITUAL AND ORDER

***The Israelites shall encamp troop by troop, each man with his division and each under his standard.** (Num. 1:52)*

A. Being orderly is an important element in perfecting oneself. A person who is disorderly in his behavior and deeds is also confused in his thoughts and incapable of stable and consistent work. A person must be orderly in all his actions. We can find a hint at the need for order from the words of our Sages, in that the head of each yeshivah was referred to as the *"raysh sidra"* — "the head of order." . . . So too do we find that the entire Torah is based on exactness and orderliness. A single second separates the Sabbath and the weekday, a hair's breadth separates the valid slaughtering of an animal and invalid slaughtering, a single drop separates a valid *mikveh* and one which is not valid, a single step separates the camp of the Levites and that of the *Shekhinah*. The Levites are forbidden to perform the functions of the *kohanim*, while the *kohanim* are forbidden to perform the functions of the Levites. Even within the Levites themselves, each is forbidden to perform the work of his fellow: *let Aaron and his sons go in and assign each of them to his duties and to his porterage* (Num. 4:19); *each man with his division and each under his standard.* (Rabbi Simḥah Zissel Ziv)

B. Whatever ethical principles you may believe in, they must have the flesh and bones of ritual to give them body, and the regularity of ritual to give them constancy. Ideals have no staying power unless they are taught continually, because life is ever conspiring through a thousand petty devices to defeat man's attempts at honesty, understanding and justice. Albert Einstein once declared: "With the affairs of human beings, knowledge of truth must continually be renewed by ceaseless effort, if it is not to be lost. It resembles a statue of marble which stands in the desert and is continually threatened with burial by the shifting sand. The hands of service must ever be at work in order that the marble continue lastingly to shine in the sun."

If it's true that "eternal vigilance is the price of liberty," it's equally true that the constant discipline of *mitzvot* is the price of religious vitality and ethical sensitivity. A musician must practice by prearranged schedule, regardless of his inclination at the moment. So with the ethical spirit. It cannot rely on caprice or chance or mood or convenience. We must labor constantly until it becomes "second nature" in the heart of man. Ritual is thus the constant instrument for giving ethical ideals a grip on our consciences. (Rabbi Robert Gordis and Rabbi David M. Feldman)[3]

These two teachings promote the value of order and discipline in religion, both as a necessity for leading a proper religious life and as a benefit thereof. And yet it is exactly this aspect of Judaism that is so difficult for some Jews, who have learned from contemporary American culture to value spontaneity and self-expression. Do you agree that "A person who is disorderly in his behavior and deeds is also confused in his thoughts and incapable of stable and consistent work" and "the constant discipline of mitzvot is the price of religious vitality and ethical sensitivity"? Why are precision and discipline as important in religion as in science? Does Judaism differ from other religions in this regard?

3. Both authors were noted Conservative congregational rabbis who were also fine scholars. Rabbi Gordis taught Bible at the Jewish Theological Seminary. Rabbi Feldman was a respected authority in Jewish law. These words are from the pamphlet "Ritual in Jewish Life," published by the B'nai B'rith Youth Organization.

THE LAYOUT OF THE CAMP: A DESIGN FOR TEACHING

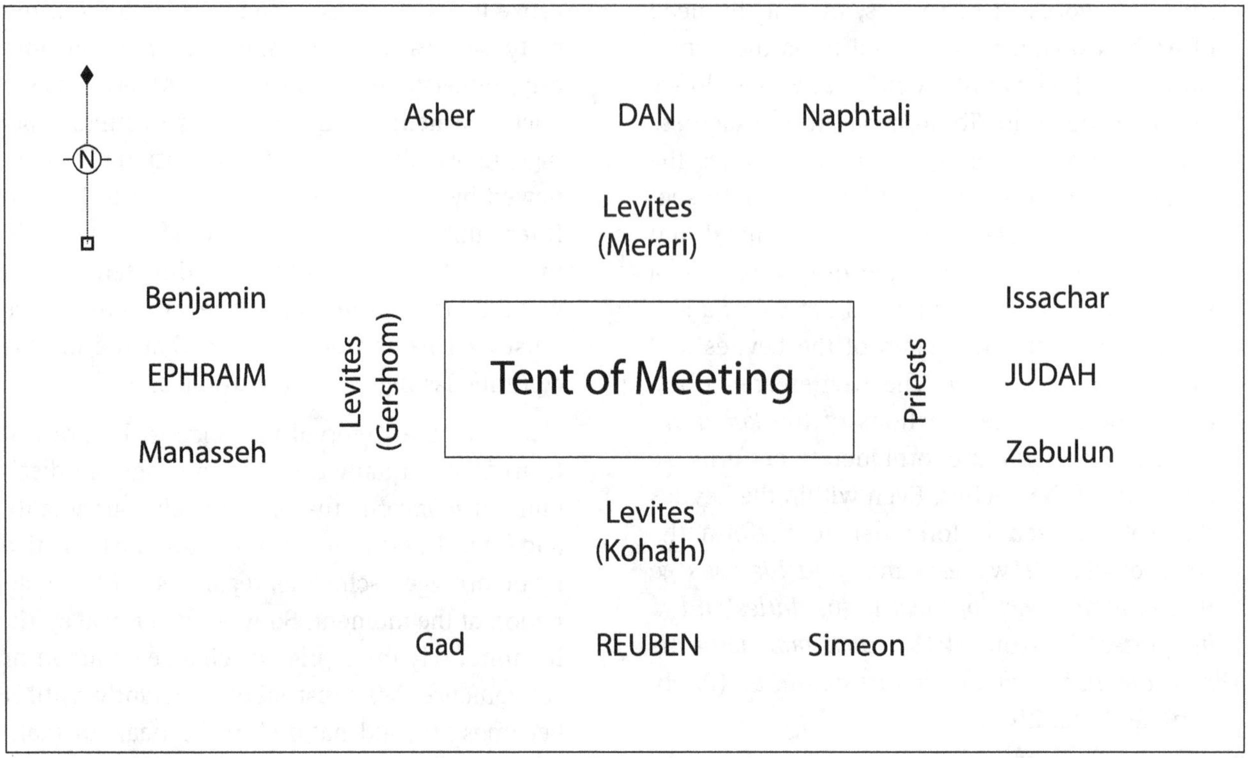

A. Ralbag holds that the east side is the most important (facing the entrance to the Tent of Meeting and the Holy of Holies), and so Moses and Aaron and his sons camped there, and likewise the royal tribe of Judah, with his younger brothers, the sons of Leah, at his side. The south side is second in importance (because the ramp to the altar faces south). There the sons of Kohat camped, whose job was to take care of the holy utensils of the Tabernacle. There also camped Reuben, the firstborn, and the tribes born after him: Simon and in place of Levi, Gad, the eldest of Zilpah, Leah's maidservant. The next level is the western side, where the Gershomites camp, who took care of the Tent and its covering, and the tribes Ephraim, Manasseh and Benjamin, the sons of Rachel. Finally, the fourth side, the north, is where the Merarites camped, who had the most difficult job (dismantling and reassembling the Tabernacle). This is also where Dan camps, the rearguard during the march and the eldest of the sons of the maidservants, with Asher, born to Leah's maidservant, and Naftali, born to Rachel's maidservant.

Abravanel explains the layout of the camp in military, strategic terms . . . Judah was placed on the east side, which is the front of the camp, who comprised, together with his brothers, 186,400 men. This is the largest encampment, good for defending against an attack. On the south and west (which are not as vulnerable) were two smaller camps: Reuben with 151,450 and Ephraim with 108,100. Nevertheless, the right side had the larger of the two camps, Reuben. Dan was on the north, the rearguard for all the camps, was the second largest camp, with 157,000 men, which is good for protecting the rear.

. . . In sum, the preparations for the Israelites' journey . . . were done according to God's command in a detailed and precise form. Attention was paid that the order be exemplary both from a spiritual point of view (the importance of each tribe, the jobs of the Levites) and from a practical point of view (military considerations). An organized camp like this, in its resting and its journeying — which in addition had to be diligent about purity and holiness so that it would be worthy for the *Shekhinah* to dwell within it — would in the future inspire wonder and awe in the nations it passed, as the verse says (Deut. 28:10), *Then all the peoples of the earth will see that the Lord's name is proclaimed over you, and they will revere you.* (Yeḥiel Moskowitz)

There are many intriguing ideas here: the balance of spiritual and mundane concerns, the attempt to match the tribe or clan with the appropriate task, the sense that everyone has something important to do, the scrupulous acknowledgment of every group, the placement of the Tent of Meeting with the Tabernacle and the Ark of the Covenant at the center. What can we learn from this about organizing our synagogues and communities? About volunteer management?

TAKING THEIR PLACES

The Israelites did accordingly; just as the Lord had commanded Moses, so they camped by their banners, and so they marched, each with his clan according to his ancestral house. (Num. 2:34)

A. Rabbi Zalman, the Rabbi of Lutzk was surprised: What was so great about this? Indeed the Sages said that Israel desired their banners and the nations of the world were jealous of them on that account. What is the wonder, therefore, that they accepted with satisfaction their hearts' desires? He answered: It was not enough that they were satisfied with the banners, but that they had no argument among them as to who would go first and who at the end, who in the East and who in the West — like what is found, to our sorrow, in synagogues and study houses — but they accepted God's word willingly and *they camped by their banners* as Moses said. *(Mi-Ma·ayanot Hanetzach)*

Anyone who has ever had to arrange seating at an event will understand immediately what this text is about. "I don't want to be at the table at the back!" "Don't you know who I am? How can you put me so far from the bima?" "I won't sit anywhere near them!" What aspect of human nature is at work here? Should we admire the Israelites, as Rabbi Zalman clearly did, for being so compliant with the mandated order, or should we be concerned that they were too regimented? Are hierarchical structures appropriate to Jewish life today?

PARENTS AND TEACHERS

This is the line of Aaron and Moses at the time that the Lord spoke with Moses on Mount Sinai. These were the names of Aaron's sons: Nadab, the first-born, and Abihu, Eleazar and Ithamar; those were the names of Aaron's sons, the anointed priests who were ordained for priesthood. But Nadab and Abihu died by the will of the Lord, when they offered alien fire before the Lord in the wilderness of Sinai; and they left no sons. So it was Eleazar and Ithamar who served as priests in the lifetime of their father Aaron. (Num. 3:1–4)

A. R. Samuel b. Nahmani said in R. Jonathan's name: He who teaches the son of his neighbor the Torah, Scripture ascribes it to him as if he had begotten him, as it says, *This is the line of Aaron and Moses;* while further on it is written, *These were the names of Aaron's sons:* thus teaching you that Aaron begot and Moses taught them; hence they are called by his [Moses'] name. (Talmud Tractate Sanhedrin 19b)

B. In other words, the passage begins by saying that it will tell the line of Aaron and Moses, but it gives only the names of Aaron's sons. This is understood as implying that since Moses was their teacher, Aaron's sons are considered as if they were his [Moses'] sons. This idea is mentioned also in the *Sifrei* on *Parashat Va-Etḥanan, "You shall teach them diligently to your children* — these are your students." And in a similar vein we find the teaching that the rabbi-teacher is called "Father" *(Av)*, as when Elisha called Elijah, *My father! My Father!* (2 Kings 2:12) *(Torah Temimah)*

C. Resh Lakish said: He who teaches Torah to his neighbor's son is regarded by Scripture as though he had fashioned him, as it is written, *and the souls which they had made in Haran.*[4] (Gen. 12:5)[5] (Sanhedrin 99b)

It is a truism that teachers are highly respected in Jewish tradition. These texts show us how greatly they are valued. Cynics might say that the Rabbis themselves were teachers, so of course they put teachers at the top. But closer examination reveals a deep truth. Remember that parents also are considered to be teachers. Think about the impact that particular teachers, particularly Jewish teachers, have had on your life. My father, who is a rabbi, told me that he once comforted a member — one who had been an active leader in the religious school — who was distraught that his son had distanced himself from Judaism. He pointed out that this man had had a positive impact on hundreds of students. It might also be instructive to compare this Jewish reverence for teachers with the attitude toward and treatment of teachers in American society.

THE FRUIT OF RIGHTEOUSNESS

And the Lord spoke to Moses, saying: "Bring near the tribe of Levi and place them in attendance upon Aaron the priest to serve him." (Num. 3:6)

A. Of them [the tribe of Levi] it is written: *The righteous will flourish*[6] *like a palm tree; he will grow like a cedar in Lebanon* (Ps. 92:13). (Midrash Numbers Rabbah 3:1)

B. There are two kinds of righteous men. One is constantly busy with his devotions and with the performance of the divine service, but does all this only for himself and not for others. He makes no effort to influence others to be righteous also. Such a man, who studies and worships for himself but does nothing to help increase the number of righteous people in the world, is like a cedar, which is a great and mighty tree but

4. This refers to Abraham and Sarah and was understood by the midrash as meaning that they converted many people to belief in one God.
5. This is a literal translation of the verse. Since, obviously, no one can make another person, these words were understood as meaning that Abraham instructed them in the understanding of God and then converted them to his new belief.
6. The Hebrew is *yifraḥ*, which means "to blossom, flower."

bears no fruit. The other is not only pious himself but also causes others to flourish in spirit, to repent of their sins and to come closer to God. He is like a palm tree, which not only grows but flourishes and yields fine fruit. The "cedar of Lebanon" only "grows" by itself, but the palm tree "flourishes"; it yields fruit, increasing the good there is in the world. The tribe of Levi was constantly engaged in the study of the Torah and in the performance of the divine service. Nevertheless, the Levites were like the palm tree in that they also took the time to study God's Torah with others and brought others closer to the ways of Judaism. (Baal Shem Tov)

Modern culture encourages us to privatize our religious life. Many Jews observe mitzvot, but they don't like to talk about it. People don't want to seem to be coming on too strong. "You leave me alone and I'll leave you alone" is the credo of modern life. Yet think how effective it would be if those who observe Shabbat, keep kosher, attend services, give to tzedakah, help the needy, etc., were to invite others to share their experience and learn from them. The example and enthusiasm of a fellow Jew is worth hundreds of sermons. What mitzvot are you passionate about? How could you help them "blossom"?

THERE IS NO SPECIAL PRIVILEGE IN THE PALACE OF THE KING

And the leader of the leaders of the Levites was Eleazar the son of Aaron the priest, in charge of those attending to the duties of the sanctuary. (Num. 3:32)

A. It was taught: R. Yehoshua ben Levi said: Elazar was a chief officer [of the Levites]. Rabbi Yehudah Berabbi says: He was an *amarkal* [counsellor, officer]. Why was he called *"amarkal?"* Because he was master *[mar]* of all *[kol]*, in spite of which, there is no special privilege in the palace of the King. (Jerusalem Talmud Shabbat 10:3)

B. This comes to explain an apparent difficulty: since he was the chief officer, great and greatly honored, why did they give him so much work, as is written in the next chapter (vs. 16), *Responsibility shall rest with Elazar son of Aaron the priest for the lighting oil, the aromatic incense, the regular meal offering, and the anointing oil — responsibility for the whole Tabernacle and for everything consecrated that is in it or in its vessels?* Is it not the way of the world to lighten the work load on a high-ranking and honored official? The explanation is "there is no special privilege in the palace of the King," meaning the Tabernacle. *(Torah Temimah)*

Why should more authority and honor require more work and responsibility? Should this be particularly true of holy work, or does it also apply to any kind of authority? Why are there no "honorary" positions in the Tabernacle? Does this translate to Jewish communal life today? What commitments should we expect from communal leaders? How about business managers and executives? Should we also expect them to "get their hands dirty?"

THE HOLINESS OF THE ARK

At the breaking of camp, Aaron and his sons shall go in and take down the screening curtain and cover the Ark of the Pact with it. They shall lay a covering of dolphin skin over it and spread a cloth of pure blue on top; and they shall put its poles in place. (Num. 4:5–6)

A. *Ark of the Pact* — (Hebrew *aron ha-edut*) "The Pact," with the definite article, can only mean the two tablets of the Decalogue that were deposited in the Ark. In the ancient Near East, important documents were deposited at the feet of the gods to indicate their authority and guarantee. In Israel, too, the Ark was conceived as God's footstool or the pedestal of His throne. (Rabbi Jacob Milgrom)

B. If the representatives of a town sell the town square,[7] they must use the proceeds to purchase a synagogue. [If they sell] a synagogue, they must purchase an ark; an ark, they must purchase wrappings [for the Torah scrolls]; wrappings, they must purchase Books [of Scripture, i.e., Prophets and Writings]; Books [of Scripture], they must purchase a Torah scroll. (*Mishnah Megillah* 3:1)

C. The Holy Ark in the synagogue, which corresponds to the Holy of Holies and the Ark of the Covenant in the Temple, is the focus of holiness in the synagogue, because it contains the most sanctified object of all — the Torah scroll. For this reason, those who are in the synagogue take great care not to turn their backs to it, so that even when moving away from it, they do so by stepping backward or sideways . . . It is a widespread custom for individuals to enter the synagogue when no prayers are being conducted, and to stand as close as possible to the Holy Ark to offer a private prayer for their personal sorrows and tribulations, or to express heartfelt thanks. (Adin Steinsaltz, *A Guide to Jewish Prayer*)

There is an etiquette, if you will, of how to behave around the Ark. Let's ponder for a moment the meaning of the two practices detailed here. How does behavior, even custom, shape attitudes and belief? Rabbi Herbert Rosner, my teacher when I was in seventh grade Hebrew school, taught me never to put a holy book on the floor and to kiss it if I dropped it. This had a lifelong impact on me. In the texts before us, we see that the proceeds of the sale of a holy article must be used to purchase an article of greater holiness. The list goes in ascending order, with the holiest thing being the Torah scroll. Parshat B'midbar always is read on the Shabbat before Shavuot, when we stand again at Mount Sinai and we encounter holiness. How can these texts help us to renew and refine our sense of awe and reverence through the way we behave in the synagogue?

HANDLE WITH CARE!

The Lord spoke to Moses and Aaron, saying: Do not let the group of Kohatite clans be cut off from the Levites. Do this with them, that they may live and not die when they approach the most sacred objects: Let

7. The town square had a measure of holiness because sometimes there were public gatherings to worship there, such as on a public fast day.

Aaron and his sons go in and assign each of them to his duties and to his porterage. But let not [the Kohatites] go inside and witness the dismantling of the sanctuary, lest they die. (Num. 4:17–20)

A. *But let not [the Kohatites] go inside and witness the dismantling of the sanctuary* — God warned against their coming to see the holy vessels when they were unwrapped and uncovered, lest it occur to them to make light of them. (Tz'ror HaMor)

B. None was allowed to choose his own article; the Kohen assigned it to him. Thus, when the Kohen covers the sacred articles the Kohatites will not push in to see in order to precede the others, and (thereby) they won't conduct themselves in a frivolous fashion, bringing the death penalty upon themselves. (Sforno)

C. At first, whoever [of the priests] who wanted to remove [ashes] from the altar did so. When there were many, they ran and went up the ramp, and whoever preceded his colleague [to the top of the ramp], won . . . Once it happened that two were even as they ran up the ramp, and one of them [realizing that he was losing] pushed his colleague so that he fell and broke his leg! Once the Court realized that there was a danger, they ruled that [the priests] would only remove the ashes from the altar by lottery. (*Mishnah Yoma* 2:1–2)

All of these comments seem to be about dangers and temptations of religious leadership. In the first case, why might the Kohatites treat the sacred vessels irreverently if they frequently saw them uncovered? In our day, how can we preserve a sense of awe and mystery in our encounter with familiar worship spaces? In the other two texts, you could view the motivation unfavorably as a competition for honor, or favorably as eagerness to experience holiness, but either way this striving clearly is problematic, more than just the risk of a broken leg. What is the danger of the kind of competition described in the second and third texts?

Parshat Naso
Numbers 4:21–7:89

Parshat Naso is the longest Parshah in the Torah: 176 verses. This corresponds to Psalm 119, the longest chapter in the Bible — also 176 verses. Furthermore, Babylonian Talmud Tractate Bava Batra is the longest tractate in the Talmud, and it is 176 pages long!

1. (4:21–49) The continuation of the census of the Levites begun in Parshat B'midbar, and their responsibilities in serving at the Tabernacle.
2. (5:1–4) A short list of certain ritually impure individuals who were to be exiled from the camp.
3. (5:5–10) Laws of theft and restitution.
4. (5:11–31) The laws of the unfaithful wife, the sotah, and the testing ordeal to which she was subjected.
5. (6:1–21) The laws of the Nazirite, a person who took a vow to accept extra restrictions upon himself: abstaining from alcoholic beverages, not shaving or cutting his hair, and other extra ritual purity restrictions.
6. (6:22–27) The Priestly Blessing.
7. (7:1–89) The *Nesi·im,* the chieftains of each of the twelve tribes, bring a joint gift, carts and oxen for the transportation of the Tabernacle when it is disassembled for travel. Then, on 12 consecutive days, they each bring identical gifts for the Tabernacle.

AGE THIRTY FOR STRENGTH

So Moses, Aaron, and the chieftains of the community recorded the Kohatites by the clans of their ancestral house, from the age of thirty years up to the age of fifty, all who were subject to service for work relating to the Tent of Meeting. (Num. 4:35)

A. From here it has been inferred that "at thirty a man attains his full strength." (*Midrash Bemidbar Rabbah* 6:7, quoting Pirkei Avot 5:24)

B. During the years of wandering in the wilderness, an Israelite at twenty was considered "able to go to war" (Num. 1:2–3). Yet, . . . the Levites began their training at twenty-five and actual service at thirty. And their work in the *Mishkan* was to take this Tabernacle apart when the time came to travel, carry the pieces, and set it up again at their next stopping-point. They needed muscles. So it would seem that seasoned strength, particularly the kind that endures, reaches its peak in a man when he turns thirty. (*Ethics from Sinai*, Irving Bunim)

C. That is, at age 30 a man has his full physical strength, and he should watch out lest he squander it on anything save the service of the Lord. (Meiri)

D. When a man is thirty, he has the strength to admonish the wicked and set them on the right path. *(Midrash Sh'muel)*

Here we have some differing ideas about what constitutes "strength," particularly mature moral strength. The third text talks about squandering one's strength. What would be some examples? Why is strength required for the task of setting the wicked on the right path? What traits and behaviors are most likely to be effective in reaching or correcting someone?

EVERY SIN IS ONE OF THEFT

The Lord spoke to Moses, saying: Speak to the Israelites: When a man or woman commits any wrong toward a fellow man, thus breaking faith with the Lord, and that person realizes his guilt, he shall confess the wrong that he has done. He shall make restitution in the principal amount and add one-fifth to it, giving it to him whom he has wronged. (Num. 5:5–7)

A. *Thus breaking faith with the Lord* — Hebrew *lim·ol ma·al be.* Rather, "whereby he commits sacrilege against." There are two prerequisites for this crime: defrauding his fellow and committing sacrilege against God by means of a false oath. (Jacob Milgrom, *JPS Torah Commentary*)

B. Why is the commandment to confess, which is the foundation for repentance for every sin, mentioned specifically here, in regard to theft? The reason is because deep down every sin is one of theft: God gave life and power to humanity, so that they should use them to do God's will, and if they use their lives and powers to transgress God's commandments, they are stealing from their Creator. That is why the Torah mentions the commandments of confession and repentance here. *(Ḥidushei ha-Rim)*

C. My grandfather[8] taught that the mitzvah of teshuvah is based on the verse, *he shall confess the wrong.* But this verse is written in connection with theft. Every transgression, he taught, is a sort of theft. One who restores everything to God, the source of life, recognizes God's mastery over all Creation. Such a person will be free from sin. *(S'fat Emet)*

D. Reverence for God is shown in our reverence for human beings . . . Human life is holy, holier even than the Scrolls of the Torah. Biblical piety may be expressed in the form of a supreme imperative: Treat yourself as a symbol of God. To meet a human being is an opportunity to sense the image of God, the presence of God. (Abraham Joshua Heschel)

8. The *S'fat Emet* is a major work by Yehudah Aryeh Leib Alter; his grandfather was Rabbi Yitzchak Meir Alter, author of *Ḥidushei ha-Rim.*

There are two types of me·ilah [the noun for the offense discussed here]: one is embezzlement, misappropriating someone else's property; the other is misuse of sacred objects or funds pledged to sacred use. For example, if you had pledged to donate a lamb to the Temple, to then use it for your own benefit was me·ilah. So, misuse of others' property and maltreatment of another human being are equivalent to me·ilah, the misuse of sacred property. What prevents this? Taking to heart the meaning of adam nivra b'tzelem Elohim (human beings were created in God's image), as Heschel helps us to understand it. We also find in the comment of the Ḥidushei ha-Rim the fascinating concept that our lives and abilities are a gift from God, and to the extent that we do not live at the highest level, we are squandering that gift. The S'fat Emet also said, "God gave the earth to humankind so that humanity can elevate it to the loftiest heavenly spheres." We find here a positive view of human nature. Some religious systems begin with the assumption of human depravity. Judaism assumes that "humanity were created in the image of God." However, though one might think that this would lead to an excessively optimistic view of human nature, in fact this view is extremely demanding — because Judaism asks us to live up to that potential. That's what the text here tells us: Our God-given abilities should not be used for evil, for doing wrong is "stealing" from God, misappropriating Divine treasures. Take yourself in your mind through a typical week and apply this test. How might you succeed and fail to meet this standard? Example: God gave me the power of speech, and I used it to gossip.

REHABILITATION AND REPENTANCE

The Lord spoke to Moses, saying: Speak to the Israelites: When a man or woman commits any wrong toward a fellow man, thus breaking faith with the Lord, and that person realizes his guilt, he shall confess the wrong that he has done. He shall make restitution in the principal amount and add one-fifth to it, giving it to him whom he has wronged. (Num. 5:5–7)

A. The penalty for apprehended theft is double the value of the stolen article (Exod. 22:3) or more (Exod. 21:37). The intent of the sharp reduction of this penalty here to 20 percent is to encourage the voluntary surrender of the theft. It is found in ancient near Eastern practice and in rabbinic law, where it is called *takkanat ha-shavim*, "a dispensation for the repentant." (Jacob Milgrom, *The JPS Torah Commentary*)

B. Another interesting example [from Israeli law] of a statute adopting the basic content of Jewish law, this time in the area of criminal law, is the Crime Register and Rehabilitation of Offenders Law, 1981. This statute regulates the recording of convictions, sentences, and other dispositions of criminal cases, and the procedures for disclosing such information. In addition, the statute includes provisions having "a social purpose of encouraging rehabilitation of penitents" by making it possible to prevent the disclosure of information about prior convictions and to expunge criminal records after the expiration of certain prescribed periods. This possibility of expunction, "as if the conviction had never occurred," is based on the Jewish concept of repentance, as indicated in the Hebrew title of the statute, *Takkanat ha-Shavim*, a halakhic term connoting assistance to the criminal offender in achieving repentance and rehabilitation. On this point, the Explanatory Notes to the bill stated:

"The basic principle upon which this bill rests is that, with certain exceptions, one should not be stigmatized all one's life because of a transgression but should be given the opportunity to turn over a new leaf; rehabilitation and full integration into society should be encouraged . . . In this connection, Hai Gaon, the head of the yeshivah in Pumbedita approximately a thousand years ago, wrote in one of his responsa: 'The law is clear that nothing can stand in the way of repentance; God forgives every penitent who He knows has regretted his ugly deeds and has resolved not to commit them again. Although human beings do not know what is hidden but only that which has been openly revealed, if a long period of time has passed and the offender has given no indication of covert or overt impropriety, and it is truly believed that he has repented, he is to be welcomed back in good standing.'" (Menachem Elon, *Jewish Law: History, Sources, Principles*)

Elon makes it clear that there are exceptions to this law. He also quotes Minster of Justice Moshe Nissim as saying, when the bill was introduced, "I must emphasize the difficult challenge this legislation puts before us, namely, achieving the correct balance between the requirements of the rehabilitative approach, which is based on the needs of the individual, and the protection of the public interest, which demands the setting of limits, harsh by their very nature, that to a certain extent are inconsistent with the approach that stresses the needs of the individual." What exceptions should there be? Does our society allow people to repent and rehabilitate themselves? What role do politics and the media play in keeping people's past offenses before the public, even when they have "paid their debt to society?"

VIDUI — THE DEATH BED CONFESSION

When a man or woman commits any wrong toward a fellow person, thus breaking faith with the Lord, and that person realizes his guilt, he shall confess the wrong that he has done. (Num. 5:6)

A. R. Nathan says: *He shall confess the wrong that he has done* — This is the precedent for the necessity of confession before death. (Sifrei)

B. The reasoning here seems to be that whoever wants to repent must confess, therefore since a person before his death certainly wants to repent, for *There is no righteous person in the world who does [only] good and never sins* (Eccles. 7:20), obviously one must confess before one's death, "for if not now, when?" *(Torah Temimah)*

C. If a person is near death, we say to him, "Confess!" And we tell him, "Most of those who confessed did not die, and many who did not confess died. Many who are walking the streets recited the confession, and in reward for confessing, you will live. Whoever confesses has a portion in the World to Come." (*Shulḥan Arukh Yoreh Dei·ah* 338:1)

D. Only if he is near death do we tell a person to recite the confession. If he is not near death, we do not do so, lest we "break his heart." (Baḥ)

E. My God and God of my ancestors, accept my prayer; do not ignore my supplication. Forgive me for all the sins which I have committed in my lifetime. I am abashed and ashamed of the wicked deeds and sins which I committed. Please accept my pain and suffering as atonement and forgive my wrongdoing, for against You alone have I sinned.

May it be Your will, O Lord my God and God of my ancestors, that I sin no more. With Your great mercy cleanse me of my sins, but not through suffering and disease. Send a perfect healing to me and to all who are stricken.

Unto You, O Lord my God and God of my ancestors, I acknowledge that my life and recovery depend upon You. May it be Your will to heal me. Yet if You have decreed that I shall die of this affliction, may my death atone for all sins and transgressions which I have committed before You. Shelter me in the shadow of Your wings; grant me a share in the world to come.

Father of orphans and Guardian of widows, protect my beloved family, with whose soul my own soul is bound.

Into Your hand I commit my soul. You have redeemed me, O Lord God of truth.

Hear, O Israel: the Lord is our God, the Lord is One.

Adonai is God. Adonai is God.

(A Rabbi's Manual)[9]

Many Jews are not aware that we have a form of deathbed confession. Why does Jewish law warn us to be very careful about when and how to offer this confession? What is the danger? What do you think about the idea of "may my death atone for all my sins"? Does that seem to be too lenient? If you were in the last moments of your life, would this confession comfort you or not?

HOW TO TREAT THE CONVERT

If the man has no kinsman to whom restitution can be made, the amount repaid shall go to the Lord for the priest — in addition to the ram of expiation with which expiation is made on his behalf. (Num. 5:8)

A. Here, you see, Scripture writes down again the section dealing with a person who robs by violence from another, and swears falsely regarding it, — it is the same section that has already been stated in *Parashat Vayikra* (Lev. 5:21), *When a person sins and commits a trespass against the Lord by dealing deceitfully with his fellow in the matter of a deposit or a pledge, or through robbery, or by defrauding his fellow,* etc. The reason it is repeated here is because of two new points contained in it. . . . [One of which is that] if something is stolen from a convert [who died without heirs, and had no extended Jewish family], the restitution must be paid to the priests [in effect, giving the restitution to God, for it was assumed that no born Jew would be without Jewish relatives to inherit the restitution]. (Rashi)

B. Tradition teaches that this verse refers to robbery of a convert, for indeed, if one robs him he profanes the Name of his God in the eyes of the convert who came to find protection under His wings. Therefore he is called "one who breaks faith with the Lord," and is required to bring a guilt offering, as is the law regarding all who trespass against Him. (Sforno)

C. The Blessed Holy One loves converts exceedingly. We likewise should show favor to the convert who left his family, his father's house, his people, and all the gentile peoples of the world, and came to us. He therefore deserves special protection. (*Midrash Numbers Rabbah* 8:2)

9. Edited by Rabbi Jules Harlow, published by the Rabbinical Assembly. There is also a form of the confession that can be recited by another on the dying person's behalf if the person is unconscious.

Why is it particularly blameworthy for a Jew to wrong a convert? One of the applications of this prohibition is that we are forbidden to remind the convert of his past, or even to refer to her as "the convert." Another form of harassing the convert is found in the Jew who delights in telling the prospective convert all the negative things (as they see it) about being Jewish. Today most synagogues have many members who are Jews by Choice. Should there be public ceremonies of welcome after someone has converted to Judaism, or would that be in the category of reminding a convert of his past? Should converts be called to the Torah as ben/bat Avraham Avinu [son/daughter of Abraham our ancestor], which calls attention to their status, or just as ben/bat Avraham? What things could we do that would fulfill our obligation to "show special favor to the convert"?

THE SOTAH: DEALING WITH A TROUBLING TEXT

The man shall bring his wife to the priest. And he shall bring as an offering for her one-tenth of an ephah of barley flour. No oil shall be poured upon it and no frankincense shall be laid on it, for it is a meal offering of jealousy, a meal offering of remembrance which recalls wrongdoing. *(Num. 5:15)*

A. Who is being reminded of wrongdoing here? Clearly it is the husband, for the minchah [meal offering] is referred to as a *jealousy* offering, not a "straying" offering, even when the priest places it in the woman's hands (Num. 5:18). The jealous husband must bring an offering because of the gravity of the situation of making such an accusation against his wife. The burden of proof, and hence, the sacrificial requirement are incumbent on him. Although he brings the offering "for her," that is, on her account, the behavior necessitating it is his.

This is also made clear by the last line of the entire section on *sotah:* "The man will be cleansed of his wrongdoing *[avon]*, and the woman will carry *[tisa]* her wrongdoing" (Num. 5:31). If she is guilty, she has sinned and is punished. However, if she is innocent, he has sinned and must make atonement.

The law of *sotah* was not so much designed to punish unfaithful wives, although it did; it was primarily intended to protect innocent women from possessive, abusive husbands who were consumed by irrational fits of jealousy. It is wholly possible that most accused women were innocent. We have no way of knowing, but recall Rashi's statement that the copper washstand promoted domestic peace by giving the accused woman "an opportunity to prove her innocence." (Judith S. Antonelli)

Antonelli points out elsewhere that everywhere else in the ancient Near East, women had no protection against jealous accusations. "Pagan law, for an accused wife, was basically lynch law." (And there are places in the world today where this is still true.) She argues that, in context, the law of the sotah was a step up for women: "Her fate was not left to a jealous husband, a court of men, an angry mob, or a pagan river god." Do you think that this ritual (which was effectively abolished in the days of the Mishnah) can be redeemed in our eyes by this line of argument? Antonelli sees this law as condemning jealousy and male violence against women. Do you find this convincing? Or is it best to just leave this whole law alone as a problematic, premodern relic?

ONE BLESSING — MANY "SPARKS"

May Adonai bless you and keep you.
May Adonai shine His face toward you and treat you graciously.
May Adonai lift His face toward you and grant you peace. (Num. 6:24–26)

A. *May Adonai bless you and keep you* — With the blessing there must be guarding . . . May *Adonai bless* with riches *and keep you* from robbers . . . May He *bless you* with wealth and *keep you* that you may perform good deeds with it . . . Another interpretation of *and keep you* is that He will keep with you the covenant made with your forefathers; and so it says, *The Lord your God shall keep with you the covenant,* etc. (Deut. 7:12). Thus Israel are both blessed and guarded. How do we know that the Shekhinah will be among them? Because Scripture states, *May Adonai shine his face* [which] means, may He give you of the light of the Shekhinah.

B. *May Adonai shine His face toward you* — may God give you brightness of eyes.[10] . . . Another exposition: *shine His face,* i.e. with the light of the Torah; it implies: May God enlighten your eyes and heart in the Torah and give you children who will be scholars; as you read, *For the commandment is a lamp, and the Torah is light* (Prov. 6:23).

C. *And treat you graciously* — May God grant you knowledge so that you may be gracious to one another and compassionate to one another; in accordance with the context, which says, And *He will grant you mercy,* etc. (Deut. 13:18).

D. *May Adonai lift His face* — But what of the text that reads, *He lifts up no face (in favor) and takes no bribe* (Deut. 10:17)? R. Jose b. Dostai expounded: How can these two verses be reconciled? In this way, *Adonai will lift up his face* in a matter that concerns you and Him, but *He lifts up no face* in a matter that concerns you and your neighbor. (Midrash Numbers Rabbah 11:5)

There are many gems of interpretation in this extended commentary from the midrash. Two to focus on are the comments on "bless you and keep you" and on "and treat you graciously." "With the blessing there must be guarding." In other words, part of the blessing is that it will be secure, protected. The first of the two comments on this is obvious: May I be wealthy and may my wealth be safe from harm. But the second is "May He bless you with wealth and keep you that you may perform good deeds with it." How does doing good with your wealth protect it? Likewise "and treat you graciously" is understood as meaning that God will give us the understanding to be gracious and compassionate to others. Usually "blessing" is understood as God granting material abundance and well-being. But here we have another understanding of blessing. What is it? Is this something worth praying for? Is the capacity for compassion and goodness something we want God to give us, or is it something we should develop for ourselves?

THE BLESSING OF SHALOM

May Adonai lift His face toward you and grant you peace. (Num. 6:26)

10. Happiness, for when someone is happy his eyes shine.

A. *Shalom:* 1) Completeness; 2) Safety, soundness, security; 3) Welfare, health, prosperity; 4) Peace and quiet, tranquility, contentment; 5) Peace, friendship; 6) Peace from war. (*Hebrew and English Lexicon of the Old Testament,* Brown, Driver and Briggs)

B. Rabbi Elazar Hakappar said: Great is shalom, for the seal [the concluding formula] of the Prayer [the Amidah] is shalom, and the seal of the priestly blessing is shalom. (Num. Rabbah 11:7)

C. The conclusions of:

The Amidah: "Praised are you, Lord who blesses His people Israel with shalom."

The Kaddish: "The One who brings shalom to His universe will bring shalom to us and to all the people Israel. And let us say: Amen."

The Grace after Meals: "May the Lord grant His people strength; may the Lord bless God's people with shalom."

The Mishnah: "R. Simon ben Halafta said: The Blessed Holy One found no vessel which could hold Israel's blessing except shalom, for it is written, 'May the Lord grant God's people strength; may the Lord bless God's people with shalom.'"

D. God pours out all kinds of blessings upon you, provided that you prepare the vessel to hold them. What is the vessel? Peace, that there be no jealousy and hatred between you. (Rabbi Mordecai Hacohen)

E. Though people are well aware of the importance of peace, they find it difficult to remain on good terms with people who constantly anger them. Respond to them, "If it were a simple matter, the Blessed Holy One would not reward peace so greatly." *(Pele Yo·etz)*[11]

Peace means more than just the absence of conflict. It means wholeness, completion, perfection in social relations. Why is peace the ultimate blessing? Why did the Rabbis construct our worship such that so many prayers conclude with a plea for peace? Think of Rabbi Hacohen's metaphor: "If there is no peace, holding on to God's blessings will be like trying to catch rain without a vessel to contain it, with just your bare hands." What must we give, what must we sacrifice, to make peace in our families, in our synagogues, in our communities? One hint comes from Pirkei Avot 1:18: "The world rests on three things: on Justice, on Truth, and on Peace."

THE BURDEN OF HOLINESS

Moses took the carts and the oxen and gave them to the Levites . . . But to the Kohatites he did not give any; since theirs was the service of the [most] sacred objects, their porterage was by shoulder. (Num. 7:6,9)

A. *Since theirs was the service of the [most] sacred objects* — Their burden was holy things such as the Ark and the Table, therefore they carried them on their shoulders. (Rashi)

B. *But to the Kohathites he did not give any* — R. Nathan says: David missed the implication of this text, for the Levites [of his day] carried the ark in a new cart; as it says, *And they set the ark of God upon a new cart,* etc. (2 Sam. 6:3); *And David was displeased, because the Lord had broken forth upon Uzzah* (ibid. 8)[12]. Ahitophel

11. "Wondrous Advisor," an ethical treatise by Rabbi Eliezer Papo (1785–1828, Ottoman Empire).
12. In the passage in Second Samuel, the Ark starts to slip off the cart, and Uzzah tries to stop it, but in doing so he touches it and is struck dead.

said to David: Could you not have learned from your Master Moses that the Levites only carried the ark on the shoulder, as it says, *But to the Kohathites he did not give any,* etc.? Consequently David sent and had it brought up upon the shoulder; as it says: *And David called for Zadok and Abiathar the priests, and for the Levites, for Uriel, Asaiah and Joel . . . according to the ordinance . . . as Moses commanded according to the word of the Lord* (1 Chron. 25:11ff.). (*Midrash Bamidbar Rabbah* 12:20)

C. *Their porterage was by shoulder* — The work of the sanctuary — all work for any holy cause — requires extra effort. "Their porterage was by shoulder" — one must harness all one's powers to this work. One does not acquire the least spark of holiness without effort. (Rabbi Menaḥem Mendel of Kotzk)

The Rabbis here solve a nagging problem of the story of Uzzah, namely what did he do that was so terrible that he deserved to die? Their answer: David caused his death by neglecting the proper treatment of the Holy Ark. This leads to the question: Why must the holiest articles be carried on human shoulders rather than on a wagon? What do you think? The Kotzker Rebbe adds another layer of meaning: that holiness doesn't come easily. How does that square with the quick fix, instant gratification tendency of contemporary American culture? Can there be such a thing as "instant spirituality"? Malcom Gladwell has written of research that shows that the elite performers (he used the example of music, but it seems to apply to other fields) "had each totaled ten thousand hours of practice." So what does it take to become spiritually or ethically adept?

HUMILITY AND TEAMWORK

The one who presented his offering on the first day was Naḥshon son of Amminadab of the tribe of Judah . . . On the second day, Nethanel son of Tzuar, chieftain of Issachar, made his offering . . . On the third day, it was the chieftain of the Zebulunites, Eliab son of Chelon . . . (Num. 7:12, 18, 24)

A. Why is Naḥshon of Judah not described as chieftain? Why did Nethanel son of Tzuar's title not precede his name like all the other chieftains, his being a prince of Issachar only recorded as an afterthought? Possibly we see here the origin of the law that when a king prays he must keep his head bowed from the beginning of the Amidah until the end, whereas the ordinary individual needs to bow only at the beginning and end of the first blessing and at the blessing that begins with "we thank you" *[Modim anaḥnu lakh]*. The idea behind this is that the more highly placed the individual, the greater the need for him to express his humility in his relationship with God. Similarly here: since Judah was destined to represent royalty in Israel [King David was from the tribe of Judah], his title, when offering sacrifices, is omitted completely. In the case of Issachar, who represents the crown of Torah, his title is mentioned only in passing — it is not headlined. Since the other tribal heads did not have such special greatness, there was no need to show special humility by withholding their titles.

. . . The Torah summarizes all the offerings at the end [vss. 84–88], giving the total of all the components of each offering, to underline that they are *all* an integral part of the dedication of the altar. In God's eyes each component ranks equally with all the other components . . . Thus, by enumerating 12 identical offerings 12 times, instead of saying, "so and so offered the same offering as his predecessor," the Torah emphasizes the individual worth of each offering plus the fact that the function of the offerings was achieved when they were all complete. (Rabbi Moshe ben Ḥayyim Alshekh)

Notice how this ethical interpretation is built upon very small details in the text, showing us once again what acute readers our Rabbis were. Alshekh makes three points: a) the need for leaders to have humility; b) the need for every Nasi [chief] to be involved; c) the equal and individual worth of each contribution. We can derive from these teachings some applications to contemporary problems of leadership. According to this, what is the proper role of the leader? Why is humility such a necessary trait? How should a leader work with other leaders and with the group? Our tradition created lessons in humility for various kinds of leaders. What equivalents would you create for today's leaders? Relating to the second and third points, how can we evaluate (and acknowledge) people's different contributions to our organization, whether of time or money?

PERSISTENCE AND CONSISTENCY

This was the dedication offering for the altar from the chieftains of Israel on the day it was anointed . . . That was the dedication offering for the altar after its anointing. (Num. 7:84, 88)

A. We must make sure that the renewal that takes place on the day of the dedication remains with us and never loses its power. The spirit of dedication that marked the "day it was anointed" must remain with us even "after its anointing." (The Rabbi of Ger)

This is a very important and difficult religious challenge. How many people leave the synagogue at the end of Yom Kippur exhilarated and filled with good intentions for adding to their Jewish observance and learning, but fail to act on those resolutions? How can we structure our lives to help us keep the momentum from our peak religious experiences? How might our religious community help us? If you were creating a reminder app, like those for diet and exercise but for spiritual matters, how might it work?

BOUNDARIES OF RESPECT AND AWE

When Moses went into the Tent of Meeting to speak with Him, he would hear the Voice addressing him from above the cover that was on top of the Ark of the Pact between the two cherubim, thus He spoke to him. (Num. 7:89)

A. *Went into the Tent* — That is, into the outer room of the Tent, separated from the Ark by the screening veil.

B. *Ark of the Pact* — Hebrew *aron ha-eidut.* "The Pact," with the definite article, can only mean the two tablets of the Decalogue that were deposited in the Ark (Exod. 25:10–16). In the ancient Near East, important documents were deposited at the feet of the gods to indicate their authority and guarantee. In Israel, too, the Ark was conceived as God's footstool or the pedestal of His throne.

C. Moses is barred from the Holy of Holies where the Presence is enthroned on the Ark-throne. He stands in the outer shrine, his view of the Ark blocked by the veil. What holds for Moses holds, therefore, for all other humans. It has already been observed that when the priests dismantle the Tabernacle (ahead of its Levite porters), they shield their eyes from the Ark and then cover it with the upraised parokhet-veil (4:5). And even Aaron, who has no choice but to enter the Holy of Holies in order to purge it of Israel's iniquities and impurities, is expressly warned that unless he blocks his vision by raising up a cloud of incense his entry will prove fatal (Lev. 16:2,13).

Thus, the priestly writers of the Torah de-emphasized the legendary superhuman status that had accrued to the figure of Moses. Not that they denied his greatness or that he was, indeed, the greatest of men. But ever wary of subsequent veneration that might lead to a Moses cult, they took pains to underscore his mortal dimensions. (Jacob Milgrom, *The JPS Torah Commentary*)

This seems to contradict what we read elsewhere, that Moses spoke to God "face to face" (Exod. 33:11; Deut. 34:10) and "mouth to mouth" (Num. 12:8) and that he saw "the likeness of the Lord" (Num. 12:8). However, Milgrom dismisses this as exaggerated language, for it is made clear to Moses elsewhere that "you cannot see My face, for man may not see Me and live" (Exod. 33:20). Furthermore, the priestly tradition within the Torah is particularly careful not to portray Moses as having viewed the Divine Presence inside the Holy of Holies, for reasons given above. It is extremely difficult for us to capture the reverence and awe implicit in these boundaries, for we live in a culture that not only holds nothing sacred, but whose most "modern" exemplars delight in crossing any and every boundary of reverence and respect. Judaism tries to preserve this sense of the holy in many ways, including having us cover our heads in the presence of the Holy Ark, rise when the scrolls are taken out, and treat holy books of all kinds with respect (not putting them on the floor, picking them up immediately and kissing them if dropped). This principle of holiness is so important, not even Moses can violate it. There is a second reason that Moses must be like everyone else: so that there won't be a cult of Moses. That is why Moses' name does not appear in the traditional Haggadah and why his burial place is secret. Why must this be so? How would it harm Judaism if Moses were "sainted" in this way? In particular, why is it so important to emphasize that no one can violate the sacred boundaries of respect and awe?

Parshat B'ha·Alot'kha
Numbers 8:1–12:16

1. (8:1–4) The commandment to Aaron the High Priest to light the menorah in the Tabernacle.
2. (8:5–22) The purification of the Levites and their dedication to service in the Tabernacle.
3. (8:23–26) The Levites' period of service.
4. (9:1–5) The first Paschal lamb sacrifice.
5. (9:6–14) Instructions regarding the "Second Passover" a month later for those unable to observe it at the proper time.
6. (9:15–23) The cloud over the Tabernacle: to indicate when to travel and when to rest.
7. (10:1–10) Two silver trumpets used to signal various matters.
8. (10:11–34) After one year less ten days, the Israelites leave Mount Sinai and travel according to a set order.
9. (10:35–36) The two sayings called out by Moses when the ark set out and when it came to rest.
10. (11:1–3) The incident at Taberah. The people complain, and God sends fire to punish them.
11. (11:4–15) The people complain again, this time about the monotony of the manna, and demand meat. Moses despairs of leading the people.
12. (11:16–35) God sends a share of the Divine spirit into the seventy elders so that they will be able to help Moses lead the people. He also sends quail for meat. God then strikes the people with a plague out of disgust with their uncontrolled cravings.
13. (12:1–16) Miriam and Aaron speak against Moses for marrying Zipporah, a dark-skinned Midianite. God reprimands them and punishes them.

DON'T EVER CHANGE!

The Lord spoke to Moses, saying: Speak to Aaron and say to him, "When you mount the lamps, let the seven lamps give light at the front of the menorah." Aaron did so; he mounted the lamps at the front of the menorah, as the Lord commanded Moses. (Num. 8:1–2)

A. *Aaron did so* — To tell us Aaron's praises, that he did not change. (Rashi)

B. It's very difficult for someone to control his impulses and not change, not add the stamp of his own personality, but simply follow all the details of an order and fulfill it as it was given. (Rabbi Yerachmiel Dushinsky)

C. Would it occur to you to think that Aaron would change and not do as God commanded? So why praise him for not changing? — Even though Aaron rose to the highest level, to the position of High Priest, he didn't change his ways and remained as before: involved with others, making peace between friend and friend and between husband and wife. This is the "praise of Aaron that he didn't change — he didn't change himself. (R. Meir Przemysl)

D. He changed nothing from the first time that he observed this commandment, neither in his attitude nor in his emotional response to it. For 39 years he lit the menorah every day, but the work never became a bother, never became routine. The enthusiasm and awe of the first occasion was there every time, without change. (The Vilna Gaon)

"There is nothing permanent except change." That sounds like the motto of the modern world, but those words were written by Heraclitus, a 5th-century BCE Greek philosopher! Nevertheless, here we read about the virtue of not changing, in three different senses. In each of the sources, what was it that remained the same? Why is this a virtue? Can you think of other examples of Aaron's problem/challenge? When are consistency and persistence virtues, and when are they not so?

WHAT IS OUR MISSION?

The Lord spoke to Moses, saying: Speak to Aaron and say to him, "When you mount the lamps, let the seven lamps give light at the front of the menorah." **(Num. 8:1)**

A. *When you mount the lamps* — Facing the menorah, there was a slab of pure marble, more strikingly beautiful than the gold, upon which the *cohen*-priest would ascend to prepare and light the lamps. On it he would also place the . . . instruments used in caring for the menorah. This marble slab was 8½ handbreadths high and 9 handbreadths long. It is understood, then, that when the Torah said *b'ha·alot'kha* [which can be understood as "when you go up," or "when you raise up"], it was referring to the fact that the priest would have to ascend the steps of this slab whenever he wished to light the lamps.

The same word also teaches us that he had to keep on kindling the lamps until the flame rose upward [*l'ha·a lot* — to raise up].

It carries the further connotation of ascent to eminence: the scripture conveys that this mitzvah would lend eminence to the Jewish people and increase their prestige in the eyes of the nations.

God is saying to the Israelites, in effect, "It is my wish that by lighting the menorah you become a light for Me, just as I was a light for you in the wilderness" — as it is written, *The Lord went before them in a pillar of cloud by day, to guide them along the way, and in a pillar of fire by night, to give them light* (Exod. 13:21). *(Yalkut Mei-am Lo·ez)*

The comment by the Mei-am Lo·ez indicates a sense of mission for the Jewish people, who by their actions — both ritual and ethical — distinguish themselves among the peoples of the earth. In Emet Ve'Emunah: Statement of Principles of Conservative Judaism, this is expressed as follows: "For the modern traditional Jew, the doctrine of the election and the covenant of Israel offers a purpose for Jewish existence which transcends its narrow self-interest. It suggests that because of our special history and unique heritage we are in a position to demonstrate that a people that takes seriously the idea of being covenanted with God can thrive not only despite oppression and suffering, but be a source of blessing to its children and its neighbors. It obligates us also to build a just and compassionate society throughout the world and especially in the land of Israel, where we may teach by both personal and collective example what it means to be a 'covenant people, a light of nations.'" Do you feel a special obligation to be righteous, or Godly, or to act in the world in any particular way, because you are a Jew?

THE DIFFICULTY OF UNITY

Now this is how the menorah was made: it was hammered work of gold, hammered from base to petal. According to the pattern that the Lord had shown Moses, so was the lampstand made. (Num. 8:4)

A. When the Rebbe of Modzitz visited Israel for the first time, in 1925, he was received by the High Commissioner, Sir Herbert Samuel. Sir Herbert told the Rabbi, among his other remarks, that he would try to make peace and unity among all the different parties and factions in the Yishuv (the pre-state Jewish community). The Rabbi replied, "Our Sages tell us that when the Blessed Holy One commanded Moses to make the Menorah, it was very hard for Moses to understand how the Menorah was to be fashioned. And even though God pointed it out to him with His 'finger,' 'This is how the Menorah is to be made,' it was still hard for him to make it. But this is quite astonishing! God is, so to speak, the teacher and Moses is the student, and even so it is hard for Moses to grasp and understand the matter?! Rather, the Menorah was supposed to be of hammered work . . . all of one piece (Exod. 25:31), to symbolize the absolute unity of the 'united tribes of Israel,' from base, that is the lowly among the people, to petal, that is the important ones of the people. Uniting all these together was the matter that was so difficult for Moses our Teacher, for to make unity among all the factions of Israel is not at all an easy matter!" *(Al HaTorah)*

Unfortunately, this comment is self-explanatory. We make jokes about "two Jews, three opinions," but it really isn't funny nor is it a cause for pride. Communities have been split, synagogues have been damaged, and people have been harmed because of disunity and factionalism. The Pele Yo·etz writes, "Unity is the foundation of a healthy society. The Divine Presence rests on Israel only when Jews are united. Any group that wishes to accomplish its goals must be united. If each individual asserts his opinions without openness to compromise, the group will be splintered; disputes will spread like wildfire, Heaven forbid." We see this happening in the Jewish religious world today, with intolerance and factionalism increasing. As the Pele Yo·etz hints, unity does not mean uniformity. It does mean mutual respect and a focus on common goals and values. Starting with our local synagogue and community, how can we maximize unity and minimize factionalism? What kind of norms of discourse and behavior could we establish? On the larger Jewish scene, what can we do to promote ahavat Yisra·el, mutual affection among Jews?

RIGHTEOUSNESS IN THE MIDST OF PLENTY

Now I take the Levites instead of every first-born of the Israelites; and from among the Israelites I formally assign the Levites to Aaron and his sons, to perform the service for the Israelites in the Tent of Meeting and to make expiation for the Israelites, so that no plague may afflict the Israelites for coming too near the sanctuary. (Num. 8:18–19)

A. It is the usual custom of the world that if, God forbid, any sorrow or distress, injury or illness, storms upon a person, at that moment he becomes much more pious and righteous; he opens his hand and his heart very wide indeed. Therefore, the Torah hints to us *may no plague afflict the Israelites — when they come near the sanctuary.* [i.e., may it not be that they are coming to the sanctuary only because they are in distress.] But rather may they do that which is good and upright in the sight of God and humanity while they are enjoying an abundance of goodness and blessing, in the midst of plenty of joy and success. (Rabbi Meir of Primishlan)

This is a comment about "foxhole conversions," based on a "creative misreading" of the text. It can be understood two ways: First, may we do good and cling to God even when times are good, and, second, may we not find ourselves in the "foxhole," in a situation of needing to turn to God in times of trouble. The question is, do people still turn to religion in difficult times? Aren't they just as likely to turn away? How should we consider those who do become more religious in times of trouble? Could it also happen that a sense of blessing and well-being would lead a person to religion? As a rabbi, I noticed that people seldom ask "why me?" when good things happen to them.[13] Yet shouldn't that sense of being blessed be a part of our outlook?

JOY VS. FUN

And on your joyous occasions — your fixed festivals and new moon days — you shall sound the trumpets over your burnt offerings and your sacrifices of well-being. (Num. 10:10)

A. *And on your joyous occasions* — the Sabbaths; *your fixed festivals* — the three [Pilgrimage] festivals; *and new moon days* — as implied. (Sifrei)

B. *We only set up an eruv for the purpose of fulfilling a mitzvah. For example: he wanted to go to a house of mourning or to a wedding feast, or to greet his teacher or his friend who had arrived from travel, or similar purposes. Or he wanted to*

13. Perhaps related to this is a comment about Horace Greeley, variously attributed: Horace Greeley is "a self-made man who worships his Creator."

stroll on holidays or Shabbat in the orchard, for there is joy in that and that is called a mitzvah matter.[14] (*Shulḥan Arukh Oraḥ Ḥayyim* 315:1)

C. When one eats and drinks and rejoices on a festival day, he should not overindulge in wine, merriment, and frivolity, believing that the more he does of this the more he is fulfilling the commandment to rejoice. For drunkenness, excessive merrymaking, and frivolity are not rejoicing but madness and folly, and we were commanded to indulge not in madness and folly but in the kind of rejoicing which partakes of the worship of the Creator of all things. (Maimonides, *Mishnah Torah*, Laws of Repose on the Festivals 6:20)

These texts tell us two things: that observance of holidays and Shabbat is a joyous thing, and that joy is not the same as fun. As Rabbi Jonathan Sacks points out, joy, simḥah is also not the same as happiness. "Simḥah is usually translated as joy, rejoicing, gladness, happiness, pleasure, or delight In fact, simḥah has a nuance untranslatable into English, joy, happiness, pleasure, and the like are all states of mind, emotions. They belong to the individual. We can feel them alone. Simḥah, by contrast, is not a private emotion. It means happiness shared. It is a social state, a predicate of 'we,' not 'I.' There is no such thing as feeling simḥah alone." This is a deep insight into Judaism and Jewish community. Shabbat and the holidays are good examples of this. It's painful to imagine celebrating them alone, isn't it? Perhaps the best example is a wedding. During the pandemic that began in earnest in 2020, hundreds of weddings were canceled. Others took place, but with just a handful of people. Beloved friends and relatives could not attend; the simḥah couldn't be shared properly. So much of today's diversions are about individual pleasure. Ask yourself, though, what gives you simḥah?

THE REAR GUARD

Then, as the rear guard of all the divisions, the standard of the division of Dan would set out, troop by troop. (Num. 10:25)

A. The Jerusalem Talmud states the following: Because the tribe of Dan was numerous in population, it would travel at the rear,[15] and whoever would lose something, [the tribe of Dan] would return it to him.[16] There is one opinion which says that they would travel like a box [i.e., in a square formation], and he derives it from (Num. 2:17) *As they encamp, so shall they journey.*[17] And there are those who say that they would travel like a beam [i.e., in a straight line], and this opinion derives it from, *as the rear guard of all the divisions.*[18] (Rashi)

---

14. The *eruv* discussed here is not the artificial boundary around an area which makes it permissible to carry on Shabbat, but a method of making it permissible to walk a longer distance than otherwise permitted, in order to fulfill a *mitzvah*.
15. There is a question implied here: why not Judah, which was the largest of the tribes? The answer is that it was the tribe of royalty.
16. The word here translated as "rear guard," *m'asef*, literally means "collecter, gatherer."
17. According to this opinion, it was the size of the tribe of Dan which suited them to be the "gatherer for all the camps," for there were enough of them to spread out behind the breadth of the marching people and gather the lost articles.
18. According to this opinion, Dan traveled at the rear of a line of tribes, and so could gather the lost articles, unrelated to the size of his population.

B. Every person, even from the other tribes, who was not able to travel with his "flag," would gather with the flag of the camp of Dan which was last, but no one was allowed to fall further back, lest he remain alone. *(Bekhor Shor)*

C. One interpretation does not contradict the other, for the tribe of Dan did deeds of lovingkindness and returned lost property and lost souls. *(Oznaim La-torah)*

Here we see a good example of how the commentators are never content with just the plain meaning of the text. The reason that a large tribe like Dan marched in the rear probably was, as some commentators note, military — to protect the rear from attack. Our Rabbis found a moral implication as well — to be the collector and protector of straying people and property. The tribe of Dan had a duty to the rest of the people because it brought up the rear. What would be some contemporary analogies to this task? Why is this a particularly worthy role to fill?

KVETCH, KVETCH, KVETCH

The people were as complainers bitterly before [Literally: "in the ears of"] the Lord. (Num. 11:1)

A. The term *miton'nim* denotes [people who seek] a pretext — they seek a pretext how to separate themselves from following God. (Rashi)

B. [Note that it doesn't say, "were complainers," but "as complainers."] It is the way of the world that when people complain about things that they lack, real or imagined, to the extent that they say explicitly what they want, the person so empowered can calm down their complaints by filling their lack or desire. This is not the case when people complain secretly, either by secret whispers, or by keeping their complaint to themselves, going about with a sour face and a turned up nose, but no one knows what they want. In such a case, you should know that they lack nothing, but simply are looking for an excuse. They don't want anyone to fulfill their request and do what they want, for then they would have no occasion to increase disputes and to incite quarrels. *(Min Ha-torah)*

If only these texts were no longer relevant! Rashi points out that such people are merely looking for a pretext. Rabbi Hacohen notes that they didn't voice their complaint publicly, but whispered it, so that Moses and Aaron didn't hear about it — only God did. As Rabbi Zelig Pliskin puts it, "The underlying theme behind a complainer is not necessarily that he wants the situation to be improved, but that he wants to have the benefits of complaining." Why is this kind of complaining so bad? What harm does it do to families, synagogues, and societies? What can we do to protect ourselves, and our organizations, from such people? One approach is to try to get them to take some responsibility for the situation about which they are complaining. Why is that a good idea? Another approach, on a personal level, is to choose not to associate with negative people. What works for you?

WOULD THAT ALL THE LORD'S PEOPLE WERE PROPHETS!

But Moses said to him [Joshua], "Are you wrought up on my account? Would that all the Lord's people were prophets, that the Lord put His spirit upon them!" Moses then reentered the camp together with the elders of Israel. (Num. 11:26–30)

A. *Would that all the Lord's people were prophets, that the Lord put His spirit upon them!* — The Lord does not restrict His gifts to particular individuals or classes. This lesson inspired a later prophet to predict, *After that, I will pour out My spirit on all flesh; Your sons and daughters shall prophesy* (Joel 3:1). (Jacob Milgrom, *The JPS Torah Commentary*)

B. Moses' reply to Joshua will always serve to remind those who will ever be called to act as guides and teachers in Israel that the ideal goal of their endeavors must be to render their own services superfluous. All the classes of the nation must attain such a lofty spiritual level that teachers and guides will no longer be needed. (Samson Raphael Hirsch)

What are the implications of this teaching? What does it say about the Jewish idea of society, of leadership, of citizenship? What rabbinic role does it emphasize? What responsibilities does it impose on every Jew? What are the implications for lay leadership? For what a synagogue should do and be? For parenting?

A SEPARATE BOOK — TWO VERSES LONG!

When the Ark was to set out, Moses would say: Rise up, O Lord! Scatter Your enemies, And may Your foes flee before You! And when it halted, he would say: Return, O Lord, You who are Israel's myriads of thousands! (Num. 10:35–36)

A. Our Rabbis taught: *And it came to pass when the ark set forward that Moses said,* [etc.]: The Blessed Holy One provided signs above and below this section[19], to teach that this is not its place [in the Torah]. Rabbi[20] said: It is not on that account, but because it ranks as a separate Book. With whom does the following saying of R. Samuel b. Nahmani in R. Jonathan's name agree: "*She* [Wisdom] *has hewn out her seven pillars:* (Prov. 9:1) — this refers to the seven Books of the Torah"?[21] Who is the Tanna that disagrees with Rabbi? It is R. Shimon b. Gamaliel. For it was taught, R. Shimon b. Gamaliel said: This section is destined to be removed from here and written in its [right place].[22] And why is it written here? In order to provide

---

19. I.e., at the beginning and at the end. This section is preceded and followed by an inverted *nun,* which separates it from the adjoining passages.
20. Rabbi Yehudah Hanassi, editor of the Mishnah, is commonly referred to as just "Rabbi," i.e., the rabbi *par excellence.*
21. Because if you count this passage as a separate book, then the preceding and following parts of the Book of Numbers are also separate books, giving a total of 7 books in the Torah.
22. The Talmud later explains this as meaning that it properly belongs in Numbers, chapter 2, in the section dealing with the distribution of the Israelites according to their banners and their traveling arrangements. Rashi explains that in the messianic future, when all punishment will end, then it can be restored to its proper place, because the influence of the Evil Inclination will be annulled, and such passages will no longer be needed as warnings.

a break between the first [account of] punishment and the second [account of] punishment. What is the second [account of] punishment? — *And the people were as murmurers* (Num. 11: 1). The first [account of] punishment? — *And they 'moved away from the mount of the Lord'* (Ibid. 10:33), which R. Hama b. R. Hanina expounded [as meaning] that they turned away from following the Lord. (Talmud Tractate Shabbat 115b-116a)

B. "Even though the Israelites sinned, God didn't want such a great accusation against them to be written. Therefore a change was made in the order of the Torah, creating a defect in the Torah, uprooting a passage from its proper place and moving it somewhere else. Behold how great is God's love for Israel and how concerned God was for their honor which is precious to Him above all things." (Rabbi Nathan Zvi Finkel) Furthermore, God didn't choose just any passage to separate the two passages, but He chose *Va-yehi bin'so·a* in order to reveal thereby God's love for Israel. The Sages say: "The Blessed Holy One said, let us not write sorrow after sorrow, but let us write a passage of honor between them." (Yalkut Shim'oni Bamidbar 10) What is written in this passage? That the Shekhinah [Divine Presence] dwells among them. By choosing this passage, God revealed that despite their sins and despite their deserved punishment, God loves and honors them, and the Shekhinah will not depart from them, but will accompany them wherever they go. We can also take a moral lesson from this, for a person is obligated to follow God's ways. *We must learn how much a person must honor his friend: even if he sees that he does a bad deed, he should not join one deed to another,*[23] *and not refrain from loving him.* Even though he is obligated to rebuke him, he should take care not to distress or embarrass him; not only should he not humiliate him, but he should increase his honor in people's eyes. (Yaakov Beifuss)

Though these two texts are complex, they are rich in meaning and relevance. First, they are an antidote to claims that the God of the "Old Testament" is a harsh, vengeful God. You can find passages in the Book of Numbers that support that position. But here we see that the Rabbis looked at the odd placement of this passage, and learned a lesson from it about God's love even in the midst of criticism and rebuke. The Book of Numbers shows that God had many opportunities to condemn Israel as incorrigible complainers and rebels, but Divine love prevailed. Then Rabbi Beifuss teaches us that we learn here yet another instance of how we should imitate God: We should judge our friends favorably and not abandon them when they transgress. No human being should ever be written off. How can we apply this type of sensitivity to our daily lives, our relationships, in public life?

BLESSED ḤUTZPAH

The people took to complaining bitterly before the Lord. The Lord heard and was incensed: a fire of the Lord broke out against them, ravaging the outskirts of the camp. The people cried out to Moses. Moses prayed to the Lord, and the fire died down. (Num. 11:1–2)

23. I believe this means that one should not accumulate one's friend's bad deeds in one's mind so as to create an overall negative judgment of him or her.

A. R. Eleazar also said: Moses spoke insolently towards heaven, as it says, *Moses prayed to the Lord.* Read not *el* [to] the Lord, but *'al* [against] the Lord, for so in the school of R. Eliezer *alefs* were pronounced like *'ayins* and *'ayins* like *alefs.* (Talmud Tractate Berachot 32a)

Rabbi Baruch Epstein explains this as an introduction to the entire chapter, which has many examples of impudent speech by Moses, for example, "Why have You dealt ill with Your servant . . . that you have laid the burden of all this people upon me?" How can we justify this ḥutzpadik behavior? Even more to the point, why does God reward Moses with a positive response? What is it about Moses that makes his "insolence" acceptable to God? Does his frankness of address have anything to teach us about theology? About prayer? About dealing with other people?

Parshat Sh'laḥ L'kha
Numbers 13:1–15:41

1. (13:1–25) Moses sends 12 men, one from each tribe, to scout the land of Canaan, and to bring a report about the nature of the land and its inhabitants. After 40 days, the spies return, bringing spectacular examples of Canaan's produce.
2. (13:26–33) Ten of the spies report that it is, indeed, a good land, but that its inhabitants are too powerful for the Israelites to conquer.
3. (14:1–7) The Israelites panic, and despite the optimistic words of encouragement from Joshua and Caleb, they rebel against Moses and Aaron and even say they want to return to Egypt! Joshua and Caleb plead with the people not to believe the negative spies' report, to no avail.
4. (14:8–10) The continuation of Joshua's and Caleb's encouraging words to the people. As a reward for their effort, the people threaten them with stoning.
5. (14:11–45) God threatens to destroy the people, but Moses intercedes. God relents, but decrees that this generation will die in the wilderness after 40 years of wandering, except for Joshua and Caleb. A group of Israelites test God's threat by trying to attack Canaan and are repelled by the Canaanites.
6. (15:1–7) Laws concerning sacrifices.
7. (15:1–16) Laws regarding sacrifices, specifying the amounts of flour and oil required for a grain offering and the measure of wine for the drink offering that accompanied major sacrifices.
8. (15:17–21) The law of challah. A portion of the dough for bread is to be given to the priests.
9. (15:22–31) The required offering when a whole community sinned unintentionally.
10. (15:32–36) An incident of Shabbat violation for which the offender was put to death.
11. (15:37–41) The laws of *tzitzit*.

WILLFUL BLINDNESS

The Lord spoke to Moses, saying, "Send men to scout the land of Canaan, which I am giving to the Israelite people; send one man from each of their ancestral tribes, each one a chieftain among them." (Num. 13:1–2)

A. Why is the section dealing with the spies put in juxtaposition with the section dealing with Miriam's punishment?[24] To show the grievousness of the spies' sin: because she (Miriam) was punished on account of the slander which she uttered against her brother, and these sinners witnessed it and yet they did not take a lesson from her. (Rashi)

B. A profound idea is hinted at here: If a person does not wish to see the truth, nothing will help, even if one shows it to him clearly. Such a person simply has closed his eyes and cannot see. That is the stress here: these wicked men saw with their own eyes and did not merely hear of the case or read about it, and yet in spite of this they did not learn from it. (Rabbi Yisrael Morgenstern of Pilov)

This point could be extended to the whole desert generation: They saw the miracles in Egypt, they were fed every day by manna, quails, and wells that appeared by the power of God, and yet they still rebelled and doubted. This seems to be part of human nature. We know the bad consequences of some deeds, yet we are not deterred. We see other people go astray, with bad consequences, and yet we take no lesson from it. Does this relate to theories of deterrence? Does the threat of punishment or bad results alone determine people's behavior? How about medical warnings against smoking or fatty foods? What else is needed?

"DON'T SEND A MAN TO DO A WOMAN'S JOB"

The Lord spoke to Moses, saying, "Send men to scout the land of Canaan, which I am giving to the Israelite people . . ." (Num. 13:2)

A. *Send for yourself men* — It was taught: Resh Lakish said "Send for yourself" — according to **your** own judgment, as it is written (Deut. 1:22): *And you all drew near to me and said: Let us send men before us and let them search out the land for us . . . and the thing was good in my eyes* — in **my** eyes, but not in the eyes of the Blessed Holy One. (Talmud Sotah 34b)

A. It was not the wish of the Blessed Holy One that the spies should go. Why? Because the Blessed Holy One had already told them the virtues of the land of Israel. . . . While they were still in Egypt He said, *I have come down to rescue them from the Egyptians and to bring them out of that land to a good and spacious land, a land flowing with milk and honey* (Exod. 3:8). (*Midrash B'midbar Rabbah* 16:7)

B. *Send for yourself men* — It specifies "men" because our Rabbis said, the men hated the Land and were the ones who said, *Let us head back for Egypt!* (14:4), and the women loved the Land, and said, *Give us a holding among our family's*

24. At the end of the last Torah portion Miriam speaks against Moses, or more specifically, Moses' wife, and is punished for it by being stricken with leprosy. This was understood as the punishment for *lashon hara*, slander. Presumably, the spies knew about this, yet it did not deter them from giving a false, negative report about the land.

kinsmen (27:4). In which case the Blessed Holy One said, "In My opinion, according to what I see in the future, it would be better to send women who love the land for they will not defame it. But you, according to your opinion that they are fit and that they love the Land, want to send men." This is the meaning of *Send for yourself*, according to your opinion, *men*, but in my opinion it would be better to send women. *(K'li Yakar)*

There is a great deal of commentary about the incident of the spies. The first comment here shows that God is skeptical of the whole enterprise and only grudgingly authorizes it. The second explains that the very request for the reconnaissance showed lack of faith in God's promise. After all, if God tells you a place is good and fertile, what more do you need to know? The third comment, by the K'li Yakar, is the most fascinating. Based on his close reading of the text, he finds evidence that it was only the men who wanted to turn back to Egypt, while it was the women, personified by the daughters of Zelophehad,[25] who dearly wanted a portion of the Land. This is the second time that the women have been presented as more loyal and level-headed than the men, the first being the incident of the Golden Calf, when (according to the Midrash) they refused to donate their jewelry for the making of the idol. Does this ring true? Are women less likely to succumb to despair and negativity? If women had a stronger say in things, would there be less violence and more compassion in public life?

TACTICS OF DECEIT

This is what they told him: "We came to the land you sent us to; it does indeed flow with milk and honey, and this is its fruit. However, the people who inhabit the country are powerful, and the cities are fortified and very large. (Num. 13:27–28)

A. R. Johanan said in the name of R. Meir, Any piece of slander, which has not some truth in the beginning, will not endure in the end. (Talmud Tractate 35a)

B. *Will not endure in the end* — For the listeners will regard them as liars, therefore one says a true thing first in order that they will believe, and the spies for that reason began with praise of the land. (Rashi)

C. Such is the way of those who utter slander: they begin by speaking well of one and conclude by speaking ill. (*Midrash Numbers Rabbah* 16:17)

D. It is the way of those who speak slander to appear as good people, and it is the way of good people to bring good news, as it says *He is a good man, and he comes with good news* (2 Samuel 18:27). (Moshe Mirkin)

25. *The daughters of Zelophehad, of Manassite family — son of Hepher son of Gilead son of Machir son of Manasseh son of Joseph — came forward. The names of the daughters were Mahlah, Noah, Hoglah, Milcah, and Tirzah. They stood before Moses, Eleazar the priest, the chieftains, and the whole assembly, at the entrance of the Tent of Meeting, and they said, "Our father died in the wilderness. He was not one of the faction, Korah's faction, which banded together against the Lord, but died for his own sin; and he has left no sons. Let not our father's name be lost to his clan just because he had no son! Give us a holding among our father's kinsmen!"* (Num. 27:1–4)

In other words, a spoonful of truth makes the lie go down. What is the purpose of these tests? Perhaps to help us evaluate the torrent of propaganda that pours into our homes over the airwaves and into our real and virtual mailboxes. There are even websites whose sole function is to fact-check various claims, because we are flooded with so much falsehood. What are some recent egregious examples that you can think of from commercials, political ads, and more?

JEWISH SELF-ESTEEM

All the people that we saw in it are men of great size . . . We looked like grasshoppers to ourselves, and so we must have looked to them! (Num. 13:32–33)

A. When the spies said, *and we looked like grasshoppers to ourselves,* the Blessed Holy One said, "I will forgive them this remark." But when they said: *and so we must have looked to them,* God asked: "Did you know how I made you appear in their sight? Who can say that you did not appear in their sight as angels?" (*Midrash B'midbar Rabbah* 16:11)

B. This was one of the sins of the spies. All right, we can understand we looked like grasshoppers to ourselves, but *and so we must have looked to them!* So what? What difference does it make to you how you look in the eyes of others? (Rabbi Menachem Mendel of Kotzk)

These two comments give us some insight into the devastating power of negativity and pessimism. In the midrash, God forgives the spies for feeling dwarfed by the Canaanites. Their crime was in giving the most negative possible interpretation to the situation. The Kotzker Rebbe goes further: Don't worry how you appear to others. Follow the truth, keep your integrity, do what you know to be right! Discuss this proposition: Being Jewish means being different. We are a minority in North America. Unless a Jew has the ability to live with this, to develop the Jewish self-esteem necessary to say, "I don't care what people think," he or she is going to have a hard time being Jewish. A related proposition to consider: The less you worry about what non-Jews think about your Jewishness, the more you act with confidence and pride, the more they will respect you.

UNANIMITY IS NOT A VIRTUE IN ITSELF

The entire community arose and lifted their voice, and the people wept that night. (Num. 14:1)

A. It was taught: R. Yehudah b. Pazzi said: Can we read this and not be confounded? For the good (Exod. 15:1): *Then sang Moses and the children of Israel;* for evil: *The entire community arose and lifted their voice.* (Jerusalem Talmud Shekalim 1:1)

Rabbi Yehudah is reacting to the fact that the same people who joined their voices in unison to praise God and thank God for their deliverance also lifted up their voices to weep in de-

spair of God's help. How could a people who behaved so nobly in one situation respond so ignobly now? Perhaps we find here a suspicion of the community's unanimity. Talmudic law states that if a court in a capital case unanimously finds someone guilty, that person is acquitted. Why should that be so? What are the dangers of too complete and enthusiastic unanimity?

POSITIVE AND NEGATIVE PEOPLE

"The land that we traversed and scouted is an exceedingly good land. If the Lord is pleased with us, He will bring us into that land, a land that flows with milk and honey, and give it to us; only you must not rebel against the Lord. Have no fear then of the people of the country, for they are our prey: their protection has departed from them, but the Lord is with us. Have no fear of them!" (Num. 14:7–9)

A. *If the Lord is pleased with us, He will bring us into that land* — This answer is the same phrasing as the spies used. They said, *Why is the Lord bringing us* (14:3), and by this they expressed their opposition to their being brought to this land, for they feared lest they fall by the sword in war, and Joshua and Caleb reply to them, that indeed God will bring them to this land *and give it to us.* We will not fall by the sword before our enemies, but rather we will drive them out. Caleb also said, when he silenced the people, *"Let us by all means go up, and we shall gain possession of it"* (13:30). But after the people set their faces against the words, as if God hated them: *Why is the Lord bringing us?* Joshua and Caleb were forced to reply to them in the same language: *If the Lord is pleased with us, He will bring us.*

Have no fear then of the people of the country — The inhabitants of the land are not giants, not very tall people, not Nephilim, but just plain "people of the country." (Yechiel Tzvi Moskovitz)

Study the passage itself and then the commentary. The riddle here is, why does one person look at a situation and judge it positively, and another look at the very same scene and judge it negatively? What was the difference between Joshua and Caleb and the rest of the spies; between the positive people and the negative people? Consider these words of the author George Eliot: "The mind that is too ready at contempt and reprobation is, I may say, as a clenched fist that can give blows, but is shut up from receiving and holding ought that is precious." Do any of these insights help us in our work and organizational lives today?

ḤUTZPAH!

As the whole community threatened to pelt them with stones, the Presence of the Lord[26] appeared in the Tent of Meeting to all the Israelites. And the Lord said to Moses, "How long will this people spurn Me, and how long will they have no faith in Me despite all the signs that I have performed in their midst?" (Num. 14:10–11)

26. The Hebrew word is *kavod*, which in this context means, as Jacob Milgrom explains, "The cloud-encased fire that descended over the Tabernacle."

A. It is written: *The whole community threatened to pelt them with stones and the Presence of the Lord appeared in the Tent of Meeting.* [Based on the juxtaposition,] This teaches that they took stones and threw them also at [God] on High. (Talmud Tractate Sotah 35a)

There are two ways to read this startling, even shocking interpretation. One, based on Midrash Tanḥuma, is that the Presence of God surrounded Joshua and Caleb to protect them, yet the people threw stones anyway. The other is that the "them" that the people threatened to stone included God's Presence. Either way, God has it right in verse 11 — the Presence of God and a plethora of miracles don't seem to be enough to convince the people. A daily diet of miracles was not enough to win over the Exodus generation from the timidity of slavery. If miracles did not work in transforming the people, what did? Why did it take so long? What lesson can we learn from this?

GOD: SLOW TO ANGER (EREKH APPAYIM)

Therefore, I pray, let my Lord's forbearance be great, as You have declared, saying, "The Lord! Slow to anger and abounding in kindness; forgiving iniquity and transgression; yet not remitting all punishment, but visiting the iniquity of fathers upon children, upon the third and fourth generation." *(Num. 14:17–18)*

A. *As You have declared* — It was taught: When Moses went up [to receive the Torah], he found the Blessed Holy One writing [as a divine attribute]: *slow to anger,* at which he said: "Master of the Universe, [qualify it as] 'slow to anger at the righteous!'" God responded: "Even from the wicked!" Moses said: "Let the wicked perish!" God said: "The day will come when you shall require My rendering!" When the Jews sinned [through the spies], the Blessed Holy One said to Moses: "Did you not say to Me, 'Slow to anger at the righteous [but not from the wicked, such as these]'!" Moses answered: "And did You not tell me, 'Even from the wicked'!" This is the intent of *Therefore, I pray, let my Lord's forbearance be great,* ***as You have declared.*** (Talmud Tractate Sanhedrin 111b)

B. It is impossible to understand the meaning of divine anger without pondering the meaning of divine patience or forbearance. Explicitly and implicitly, the prophets stress that God is patient, long-suffering, or slow to anger *(erekh appayim)* (Exod. 34:6; Num. 14:18; Jer. 15:15; Joel 2:13; Jonah 4:2; Nah. 1:3). Patience is one of the "thirteen attributes of God," yet never in the sense of apathy, of being indifferent. Contrary to their thinking was the idea of a God who submits to the caprice of man, smiling at the hideousness of evil. The patience of God means his restraint of justifiable anger.

One must not mistake divine forgiveness for indulgence or complacency. There is a limit at which forbearance ceases to be a blessing. Forgiveness is neither absolute nor unconditional. We may forgive the criminal; is it right to forgive the crime? I may forgive a wrong done to me; but do I have the right to forgive a wrong done to others? Unconditional forgiveness may be found in Pandora's box, a fine incentive to vice. Anger is a reminder that man is in need of forgiveness, and that forgiveness must not be taken for granted. The Lord is long-suffering, compassionate, loving, and faithful, but He is also demanding, insistent, terrible, and dangerous. (Abraham Joshua Heschel, *The Prophets*)

These two teachings balance each other out perfectly. The Talmud stresses for us God's patience. Once in an adult Bible class we were studying the Prophets, and someone commented, "Boy, God really put up with a lot!" That is the quality of patience, of being slow to anger. Yet, as Heschel reminds us, too much patience is also not good. At what point does patience "cease to be a blessing?" What about Heschel's two questions? What happens to society when people are forgiven too easily? What happens to people themselves? What if there is no mechanism for seeking and gaining forgiveness through repentance and restitution? How do we find the right balance between patience with human failings and righteous and justified indignation?

DEEP REPENTANCE

When Moses repeated these words to all the Israelites, the people were overcome by grief. Early next morning they set out toward the crest of the hill country, saying, "We are prepared to go up to the place where the Lord said we have sinned." But Moses said, "Why do you transgress the Lord's command? This will not succeed. Do not go up, lest you be routed by your enemies, for the Lord is not in your midst. For the Amalekites and the Canaanites will be there to face you, and you will fall by the sword, inasmuch as you have turned from following the Lord and the Lord will not be with you." Yet defiantly they marched toward the crest of the hill country, though neither the Lord Ark of the Covenant nor Moses stirred from the camp. And the Amalekites and the Canaanites who dwelt in that hill country came down and dealt them a shattering blow at Hormah. (Num. 14:39–45)

A. R. Avraham Mordecai Alter of Gur once visited Rabbi David Goldman in Kielce, and in the course of their conversation asked him, "As our Sages tell us that the gates of repentance are never locked, why was the repentance of the Israelites, who admitted 'We have sinned,' not accepted?" Rabbi David answered, "It is true that repentance is not rejected, but that is only if the person realizes that he had sinned, regrets his action and forsakes that type of action in the future. That is true repentance. However, the Israelites of the desert generation did not say, 'We will go up because we sinned,' but rather, 'We will go up to the place where the Lord said we have sinned.' In other words, we do not admit that we sinned, but '*God said* we have sinned,' and that is why we are repenting. That is not true repentance." The Gerer Rebbe was delighted by this answer, and told those close to him, "That is the way one must learn a verse in the Torah." *(Itturay Torah)*

This story clarifies the difference between deep and superficial repentance. What was so bad about the Israelites' approach? They acknowledged that God has found their behavior wanting. They expressed regret about what happened. They tried to please God. What is it about their words and deeds in this passage that causes God to reject their plea, when God forgave them for earlier trespasses, including the Golden Calf? How might we apply it in criminal proceedings today? Should remorse make a difference in sentencing? And consider how public figures have been known to "apologize." "I'm sorry if some people were offended."

GOD'S REASSURANCE

The Lord spoke to Moses, saying: Speak to the Israelite people and say to them: When you enter the land that I am giving you to settle in, and would present an offering by fire to the Lord . . . (Num. 15:1–3)

A. This passage was juxtaposed to the preceding one [wherein they are told that their generation will die in the wilderness]. Since they had repented and were in mourning, [God] comforted them and told them that their children would settle the land. (Ibn Ezra)

B. After God promised the children that they would enter the land, He completed for them the law of the sacrifices: they would offer wine libations when they entered the Land. Perhaps this was in order to comfort them and to promise them, for they were despairing, saying: "Who knows what will be after such a long time at the end of forty years. And what if our children sin?" Therefore the Blessed Holy One saw fit to comfort them, for by commanding them laws that were to be fulfilled in the Land, God promised them that it was revealed before Him that they would enter and inherit it. (Ramban)

Here we have a very sensitive reading. The commentators asked, why does this commandment appear at this point, given that it can only be performed after the Israelites enter the Land of Israel? The answer is: Exactly! God gives this commandment precisely here to a depressed and dejected Israelite people in order to say: Though you are being punished, there will be an end to punishment, and the covenant promise will be fulfilled through your children. Why is this comfort necessary at this juncture? What is the balance between justice and mercy that is presented here?

DUE DELIBERATION

Once, when the Israelites were in the wilderness, they came upon a man gathering wood on the Sabbath day. Those who found him as he was gathering wood brought him before Moses, Aaron, and the whole community. He was placed in custody, for it had not been specified what should be done to him.[27] (Num. 15:32–34)

A. This is one of the four legal cases that came up before Moses our master. In two of them Moses was quick (to act) and in two of them Moses was tardy. And in each case Moses said: I have not heard (the like). (He was quick to act) in the case of the unclean persons who could not keep the Passover at its appointed time (Num. 9:6–13) and in the case of the daughters of Zelophehad (27:1–11; 36:1–12) because civil cases were involved. But in the case of the wood gatherer who profaned the Sabbath willfully and in the case of the blasphemer who pronounced the Holy Name blasphemously (Lev. 24:10–23), Moses was tardy because these were capital cases. This was in order to teach the judges who would succeed Moses that *they should be quick*

27. Although this harsh punishment seems excessive to us now, Jacob Milgrom explains that in the Torah's context, the public violation of the Shabbat demoralizes the community, and so must receive swift and sure punishment.

in civil cases and tardy in capital cases, so that they would not be in a hurry to put to death even one condemned to death; and so that they would not be ashamed to say: We have not heard (a similar case), since Moses our master has also said: I have not heard. *(Targum Neofiti)*

This teaching teaches us three important things: 1) Judges should complete civil cases swiftly; 2) Judges should not "rush to judgment" in capital cases; and 3) Judges should be sure of their grounding in the law when they exercise their authority. Why is each of these important? What happens to people's attitudes toward the law and the justice system when these things do not occur? Why is it particularly important that capital cases not be decided in haste? What do each of these principles have to teach contemporary society — and the American legal system — today?

DECODING THE TZITZIT

The Lord spoke to Moses, saying: Speak to the Israelite people and instruct them to make for themselves tassels [tzitzit] on the corners of their garments throughout the generations. That shall be your fringe; look at it and recall all the commandments of the Lord and observe them, so that you do not follow your heart and eyes in your lustful urge. Thus you shall be reminded to observe all My commandments and to be holy to your God. I the Lord am your God, who brought you out of the land of Egypt to be your God: I, the Lord your God. (Num. 15:37–41)

Here is a compilation of details about the tzitzit and their reasons:

Four Corners

The tzitzit are to be put on a garment with 4 corners but not on one with 3 or 5, thereby alluding to the 4 different terms used by God to describe the deliverance from Egypt, for it states (Exod. 6:6–7), *And I will bring forth, and I will deliver, and I will redeem, and I will take out.* (Rashi)

Five Knots

In order to remember the Five Books of the Torah. *(Ba·al Ha-turim)*

Reminding us of the 5 senses, indicating that they are all to be dedicated to God. (Rabbeinu Baḥya)

Eight Strings

Refer to the 8 days of circumcision. (Rabbeinu Baḥya)

Are an allusion to the 8 days that Israel waited between the Exodus from Egypt and the Song of Praise after crossing the Red Sea. (Rashi)

Five Knots + Eight Strings

The *gematria* (numerical value) of the letters of the word *tzitzit* totals 600. Add the eight threads and the five knots and you have a total of 613. *(Midrash B'midbar Rabbah 18:21)*

Thirty-nine Windings Between the Knots (7 + 8 + 11 + 13)

7 + 8 = 15, the numerical value of *yud* and *hay.* 11 = 6 + 5, the numerical values of *vav* and *hay,* which join together to make the Name of God. Then 13 forms the *gematria* of the word *echad* (1 + 8 + 4), and thus: *Adonai Echad,* "The Lord is One." *(Be·er Heiteiv)*

Welcome to the wonderful world of Jewish numerology! Why do you think our Rabbis developed so many interpretations of the various numbers of knots and strings? How can knowing them help the tzitzit function as a reminder to follow God and resist temptation?

THE TZITZIT AS REMINDER

A. From this passage we see that the purpose of the tzitzit is the purpose of all the commandments: to aid Israel in becoming holy. To be holy — in Hebrew, *kadosh* — involves both a "separation from" and a "dedication to": a separation from that which is idolatrous, spiritually contaminating, morally degrading; and a dedication to that which is Godly, spiritually purifying, and morally elevating . . . Seeing the fringes, a Jew remembers the commandments; remembering, he strives to do them. All three steps are important: the seeing, the remembering, and the doing. Yes, the *tallit*, when regularly and reverently worn, can strengthen our will and replenish our resources for resisting the temptation to do evil. (Rabbi Hershel Matt)

Is Rabbi Matt correct? Do we need reminders and techniques to help us control our impulses? Will just looking at the tzitzit alone help us keep the right path? How can kissing the tzitzit every time we read the word "tzitzit" help us to use them as a reminder?

Parshat Koraḥ

Numbers 16:1–18:32

1. (16:1–11) Korah and his faction rebel against Moses and Aaron's authority.
2. (16:12–15) Moses sends for Dathan and Abiram, who had joined with Korah, to appear before him, and they refuse.
3. (16:16–35) Moses proposes a test to Korah and his followers: offer incense before God, and see if God accepts it. After the Israelites withdraw from the rebels, the earth splits and swallows up Korah and his followers. Then a fire bursts out and consumes the 250 rebellious Levites.
4. (17:1–8) As a warning to future generations, the rebels' copper incense pans are gathered up and beaten into a covering for the altar.
5. (17:9–15) After further complaints by the Israelites, a plague breaks out among them, but Aaron quickly offers incense to expiate their sins, preventing further casualties.
6. (17:16–24) Each tribal chieftain is asked to take a wooden staff to the Tent of Meeting. Aaron's alone sprouts blossoms and almonds, proving that God favors his leadership.
7. (17:25–28) Aaron's staff is left before the Ark as "a lesson to rebels."
8. (18:1–7) The division of tasks among the priests and Levites, beginning with the assignment of the High Priesthood to Aaron and his descendants.
9. (18:8–20) Neither Israelites nor the priests will be given any tribal portion in the land. Instead, they will be supported by gifts and shares of sacrifices.
10. (18:21–32) The Levites are to receive the tithe, 10% of the people's harvest. They are then to give 10% of their tithe, also called *terumah,* to the priests.

A CONTROVERSY FOR HEAVEN'S SAKE

A. A controversy for Heaven's sake will have lasting value, but a controversy not for Heaven's sake will not endure. What is an example of a controversy for Heaven's sake? The debates of Hillel and Shammai.[28] What is an example of a controversy not for heaven's sake? The controversy of Korah and his associates. (*Pirkei Avot* 5:19)

B. In [Hillel and Shammai's] debates, one of them would render a decision and the other would argue against it, out of a desire to discover the truth, not out of cantankerousness or out of the wish to prevail over his fellow. That is why when he was right, the words of the person who disagreed, endured. A controversy not for the sake of heaven was the controversy of Korah and his company, for they came to undermine Moses, our master, may he rest in peace, and his position, out of envy and contentiousness and ambition for victory. (Meiri)

C. We frequently see that the parties in a controversy stand up to their teachers and speak to them with pride and mockery. How can one tell if their intention is to mock and scorn their teachers, or if it is for the sake of heaven? Indeed, this is how to tell: If you see that there is unity in their group and each one is joined to his fellow with great love, this is a sign that they are speaking words of truth, and their intentions are for the sake of heaven. But if we see that except for the matter of controversy that unites and connects them, in all other matters they are divided, and there is jealousy and hatred in their hearts, this is a sign that their intention is not for heaven's sake, but only the evil of their hearts brought them to this dispute. That is what Avot says here: "What is an example of a controversy not for heaven's sake? The controversy of Korah and his associates." There were 250 people, and each one of them lusted after the High Priesthood, and so we find that controversy ruled among them — [read it:] "the controversy *between* Korah and his associates," but they were all united against Moses with a unified opinion to dispute with him. (R. Pinchas Kahati, quoting *Noam Elimelekh*)

Avot here teaches us that truth can arise out of a controversy properly conducted, and that even strong words in criticism of an idea or a conclusion need not result in enmity. Two clues to tell the difference between someone who argues for the sake of truth and someone who just wants to stir up trouble: a) Is the argument on the issue? Is there any trace of criticism of the integrity or ability of the person or the group holding the other position? Is the dispute about winning or losing, or is it about the best way to do the right thing? b) Is the group initiating the controversy divided among itself? Do they maintain cordial relations with one another, as well as with those with whom they disagree?

DON'T CLING TO A QUARREL

Moses rose and went to Dathan and Abiram, the elders of Israel following him. (Num. 16:25)

28. Hillel and Shammai were two great rabbis who were important leaders and teachers in the first century C.E. They often disputed over points of Jewish law, and they founded schools of thought (known as Beit Hillel and Beit Shammai) which continued to debate.

A. Resh Lakish said: This teaches that one must not "cling" to a quarrel; for Rav said: He who is unyielding in a dispute violates a negative command, as it is written, *And let him not be as Korah, and as his company.* (Num. 17:5) (Talmud Tractate Sanhedrin 110a)

B. For he disregarded his own dignity, and he himself went to neutralize conflict. (Rashi)

C. This means that we do not allow a quarrel to take root, for if Moses had not gone to them they would have been maintained in conflict, and he tried to go to them for perhaps he would be able to quench the fire of controversy. And even according to the one who says (Kiddushin 32a), "If a rabbi renounces his honor, it is not renounced," in a situation where it is possible by means of such renunciation of honor to prevent conflict, his honor is renounced, and in fact it should be, for thus did Moses renounce his honor by going to see the inciters of the conflict. *(Torah Temimah)*

Think how many disputes, conflicts, and wars keep going because no one wants to bend; no one wants to seem weak, or lose the perceived upper hand. In other words, it becomes as much about pride as it does about principle. Here we learn that a Jew is prohibited to hold on to a quarrel. What do we lose and what do we gain when we disregard our own dignity for the sake of peace?

OUR LIVES BEAR TESTIMONY

And Moses said: "By this you shall know that it was the Lord who sent me to do all these things; that they are not of my own devising." (Num. 16:28)

A. Korah had accused Moses and Aaron: *Why then do you raise yourselves above the Lord's congregation?* He accused Moses of elevating himself and his brother and his family, as if Moses sought honor for himself and coveted greatness and power, in a situation where there is no spiritual need for such: *For all the community are holy, all of them, and the Lord is in their midst.*

Moses, in his answer, reminds the people that Korah's accusation is completely baseless. Whoever knows Moses' past knows that all his deeds and history point out his devotion to his task and his fleeing from honor and personal elevation: *I have not taken the donkey of any one of them* — I did not worry about raising my standard of living, that I should ride and they should walk. If I had lusted after kingly palaces, who forced me to abandon the royal palace, to go out to my brothers and see their suffering? Who could have made me rescue the daughters of the priest of Midian from the shepherds? Is it not so that when I stood before God at the bush and God commanded me to go to Pharaoh, to return to Egypt, I declined: Please, O Lord, make someone else Your agent, for I didn't find myself to be fit for the task.

Therefore Moses says to the people: How could you believe Korah's words that I elevate myself and covet power? Is it not so that *By this you shall know that it was the Lord who sent me*? You who know me, my character and my nature, know they are not of my own devising [literally: they are not from my heart]. For such an inclination could not come from the depths of my heart and soul, for there is no such motive in my heart, for any desire to elevate myself over others is in complete opposition to the testimony of my life. (R. Jacob Duschinsky)

This lovely comment is rich in wisdom. Why does Moses feel that he is entitled to be believed over Korah? According to this, what is the best evidence that Korah's accusations are false? If we want to be judged favorably by others, how should we conduct our lives? If someone seems to be living an upright life, how should we respond to accusations of wrongdoing? There seems to be a belief these days, fostered by the media, that every exemplary life is merely a façade masking a more sordid reality. It is taken as a challenge to find the dirt on even the most admirable public figures. What happens to relationships, public trust, and our expectations of other people when we take that view? What happens when we follow the approach that Moses presented?

LAST-MINUTE REPENTANCE

Scarcely had he finished speaking all these words when the ground under them burst asunder, and the earth opened its mouth and swallowed them up with their households, all Korah's people and all their possessions. They went down alive into Sheol,[29] with all that belonged to them; the earth closed over them and they vanished from the midst of the congregation. (Num. 16:31–33)

A. The congregation of Korah is not destined to ascend [from the earth], as it is written, *the earth closed over them* — in this world, *and they vanished from the midst of the congregation* — in the next: this is Rabbi Akiba's opinion. Rabbi Eliezer said: of them it is written, (1 Sam. 2:6) *The Lord deals death and gives life, Casts down into Sheol and raises up.* (*Mishnah Sanhedrin* 10:3)

B. It appears from his [Rabbi Eliezer's] words that they felt their sin and repented [as they fell into the pit]. (Meiri)

C. Was Moses so cruel that he wasn't content with a regular death but they had to go down alive to Sheol? But in fact Moses showed them special lovingkindness in that *they went down alive,* for if they had died immediately, without repentance, they would have been lost forever, so Moses requested that they go down alive to Sheol, so that while they were still alive they would have an interval in which to repent. That is the meaning in the Talmud of Rabbi Eliezer's statement: that the congregation of Korah also have a share in the World to Come, for they had enough vitality left to repent. (Rabbi Reuven Margalit)

Chapter 10 of Mishnah Sanhedrin has to do with the World to Come. Mishnah 3 discusses who will receive the reward of the World to Come, and it states that the Flood Generation and the generation of the Tower of Babel will not be rewarded, while there are disagreements about the people of Sodom and Gomorrah, the Desert Generation, and Korah's company. However, it seems that the majority of the sages agreed with Rabbi Eliezer that they did not suffer eternal punishment. Rabbi Margalit, in a remarkable comment, finds a hint about this in the text. One of the most important functions of the belief in an afterlife in Judaism is to preserve a sense of God's justice (since in this world the wicked often prosper and the righteous suffer). Yet Judaism

29. The underworld.

generally reserves eternal punishment only for the most wicked. What does this say about God and God's justice? Is God too lenient?

THE VALUE OF ATHEISM

Remove the fire pans of those who have sinned at the cost of their lives, and let them be made into hammered sheets as plating for the altar — for once they have been used for offering to the Lord, they have become sacred — and let them be a warning to the people of Israel. Eleazar the priest took the copper pans which had been used for offering by those who died in the fire; and they were hammered into plating for the altar, as the Lord had ordered him through Moses. It was to be a reminder to the Israelites, so that no outsider — not of Aaron's offspring — should presume to offer incense before the Lord and suffer the fate of Korah and his band. (Num. 17:2–5)

A. On a superficial level, the point is clear. The memory of Korah's rebellion must be kept alive. The Israelites need to be reminded again and again of the disastrous results of rebellion. Hence, the plating on the altar.

But I have always felt that there are much more profound implications to this text, and when I shared this intuition with a colleague he directed me to a startling essay by Rabbi Abraham Isaac Kook, "The Pangs of Cleansing," on the religious legitimacy of atheism.

Atheism, Rav Kook claims, is necessary because it stands as a perpetual reminder to the community of believers, a rebuke to the inevitable corruption that accumulates around faith and religion — the tendency to anthropomorphism, to conceive of God in narrow and unrefined ways, to concentrate on the words and letters of Torah instead of the thoughts and feelings that it expresses, and on its ultimate moral thrust. In fact, atheism's denial of the "existence" of God is totally on target, for to Rav Kook, to claim that God "exists" is to fall into idolatry. A stone can be said to exist. God, however, does not exist. God is beyond or above existence, the ultimate source of existence. Atheism, Rav Kook insists, is an instrument for repentance. It is also, thus, a necessary prelude to redemption.

The plating on the altar then is not simply a reminder of Korah's sin. It is even more a reminder of the sin that lurks in the heart of the pious, within all of us, a perpetual warning that it is not at all clear who is the saint and who the sinner, that each of us is both saint and sinner, that the line that separates the two is very murky indeed.

. . . The tension between atheism and affirmation remains within each of us at all times. Religious faith at its most authentic is precisely the dialectic between these two poles. Faith is never something we "have" totally and thoroughly at all times. We are all, rather, perpetually in process, on the move, between the polarities of affirmation and denial.

The reason for plating the altar with the pans of the rebels is to remind us of the rebelliousness that is legitimately within ourselves. For it is never clear who is the authentic believer and who the atheist; there is both believer and atheist within each of us. Even more, there is truth here that both the believers and the atheists among us might well ponder. (Neil Gillman)

We usually see atheism and theism as polar opposites that cannot be reconciled. You are either a believer or you are not. Rabbi Gillman shows us that reality is more complex. The arguments of the atheist provide a necessary counterweight to the danger of too certain a faith in God. That can lead one to assume that one knows the mind of God. As humorist Finley Peter Dunne once wrote, "A fanatic is someone who does what God would do if only God knew the facts of the matter." Consider in particular the idea that "the life of faith at its most authentic necessarily includes both moments of belief and unbelief."

KEEP FAR FROM A QUARREL

***Let him not be like Korah and his band.** (Num. 17:5)*

A. Rav said: All who nurture a quarrel break a negative commandment, i.e., *Let him not be like Korah and his band.* (Talmud Tractate Sanhedrin 110a)

B. One must keep a distance from disputes. Besides the inherent severity of this sin, it is the source of many other serious transgressions: unwarranted hatred, *lashon hara* (gossip), *r'khilut* (talebearing), anger, insults, humiliating words, revenge, grudges, curses, and *ḥillul Hashem* (desecration of God's name)

If someone finds himself in the midst of a dispute, he should withdraw immediately. Some people might feel embarrassed to back down in the middle of an argument. They should recall these words of our Sages (*Mishnah Eduyot* 5:6), "It is better for a person to be considered a fool throughout his entire life by a person, than to be considered wicked for one moment in the eyes of God."

One should not take part in a feud even if his parents are involved. Because Korah's sons refused to side with their father in his dispute against Moses, they were saved from being punished with their father.

It is a very important mitzvah to stop a feud. Even if you have tried to do so many times and your efforts have been fruitless, you should not be discouraged. There is always the possibility that next time you might be successful. (*Sh'mirat Halashon*, by the Ḥafetz Ḥayyim)

This is a further development of the commentary on Numbers 16:25. Clearly our rabbis were appalled by the contentiousness and ad hominem venom of Korah's challenge. They sought to learn from his negative example. They also knew that the destruction of the Second Temple came about because of Jewish factionalism. How do disputes lead to the other transgressions listed by the Ḥafetz Ḥayyim? The laws of behavior laid out here are quite explicit. Discuss them in detail and try to apply them to familiar situations. Are they realistic? Finally, consider this idea: "War is not a metaphor for sports. Sports are not a metaphor for life."

CREDITING BOTH SIDES

***Let him not be like Korah and his band.** (Num. 17:5)*

A. Indeed it appears that the chapter of controversy has not ended. Every generation has its controversies, its quarrels and its arguments. The explanation is that a controversy like that between Korah and Moses will not occur again, for in that quarrel the truth was all on Moses' side and all the distortion and falsehood was on Korah's side. A controversy like that was finished. "Let there not be like Korah and his company" is meant literally, that in every controversy each side has something on which to rest, there is some truth and justice on every side. The test is only which side has the greater measure of justice. (Rabbi S. Brot)

This teaching highlights the human tendency to see opponents as Korahs — with bad reasons and selfish motives for their action. This is often particularly true in religous disputes and, increasingly, in political arguments. Rabbi Brot suggests that except for Moses' and Korah's quarrel, most controversies have some measure of truth on both sides, and thus good faith on both sides. If this is generally so, what does it suggest about the ground rules for managing conflict in organizational life? What kinds of behavior and rhetoric should be "out of order"? How should decisions be made? What should happen after the decision is made?

MOCKERY CORRODES EVERYTHING IT TOUCHES

The staff of the man whom I choose shall sprout, and I will rid Myself of the incessant mutterings of the Israelites against you. (Num. 17:20)

A. *Happy is the man who has not followed the counsel of the wicked, or taken the path of sinners, or joined the company of the scoffers* (Ps. 1:1) — This refers to Korah who mocked Moses and Aaron. What did he do? He assembled the whole community and began to speak words of mockery before them. *(Yalkut Shimoni)*

B. Forming the third category in this cast of dishonorable characters are the "scoffers," in Hebrew *letzim* [sing. *letz*]. This term is also variously rendered in the English translations by "the scornful," "the mockers," "the cynics," all designations richly deserved by these people. Very frequently, the *letzim* are associated with the foolish, the arrogant, and the wicked. This should not be surprising because in the Bible, folly is less a condition of intellectual inadequacy than a lack of discrimination and judgment in the moral sphere — the inability or unwillingness to foresee or consider the consequences of one's actions. A close look at the passages that refer to the *letz*, overwhelmingly in the Book of Proverbs, shows that the one so described is outrageously and proudly insolent, is a menace to the social order, and is incorrigible, reacting abusively and hostilely to any reproof; he is described as "an abomination to humankind." Other derivations of the same Hebrew stem that underlies *letz* indicate that these types indulge in mocking poems and satires that deride the traditional values that society cherishes and taunt those who uphold them. (Nahum Sarna, commenting on Psalm 1)

Rabbi Ya'akov Beifuss, in his collection of comments on the weekly Torah portion Yalkut Lekaḥ Tov, suggests that it is the power of mockery that explains why the test of the blos-

soming staff was not conducted until after Korah and his band are destroyed. "Korah was clever, and he knew that by means of rational argument he would not be able to get the people to rebel, for in a war of intellect Korah certainly would not be able to defeat Moses. Therefore he used the weapon of mockery, for one act of mockery cancels a thousand rebukes." It was only after the mockers were destroyed that the stupidity, blindness and deafness produced by the mockery was removed, and the people could really see the results of the test, proving Aaron's authority. Samuel Johnson said that ridicule is "A kind of gangrene, which if it seizes one part of a character corrupts all the rest." Mockery tempts us because it makes us feel superior to the target. No one wants to appear foolish, so few stand up to the scornful. Think about how much of the humor in our time mocks and ridicules the common decency and simple piety of ordinary people. What is the impact of this on us? How can we resist the corrosion of this destructive and condescending form of humor?

LIMITATION OF PRIESTLY POWER

[God to Aaron] I hereby take your fellow Levites from among the Israelites; they are assigned to you in dedication to the Lord, to do the work of the Tent of Meeting. (Num. 18:6)

A. *In dedication to the Lord* — "To the Lord" they are given, and not to the priests. *(Sifrei)*

B. That is to say, they are not given to the priests in order to serve *them* by doing their personal, secular labor, but only in connection with the holy labor, the work of the Tent of Meeting. *(Torah Temimah)*

And the Lord said to Aaron: You shall, however, have no territorial share among them or own any portion in their midst; I am your portion and your share among the Israelites. (Num. 18:20)

C. Even though the Torah recognizes that the priests have certain superior qualities, it did everything possible to prevent them and the Levites from controlling the other tribes. In Egypt, for example, all land belonged to Pharaoh, except for the priests' land, even though they received an allotment from Pharaoh's house (see Genesis 47:22–26). In Israel, the exact opposite was true: All the tribes were given their own land in Eretz Yisrael, and it was the tribe of Levi, including the priests, which did not receive any land, for "God is his inheritance." (Hillel Zeitlin)

What are the dangers of combining religious authority with temporal power and wealth? Is this still a problem today? On another level, what's wrong with the priests using the Levites for their own personal work? What would be analogies today in the workplace? In the political arena?

PIDYON HA-BEN / REDEMPTION OF THE FIRST BORN

The first issue of the womb of every being, man or beast, that is offered to the Lord, shall be yours; but you shall have the first-born of man redeemed, and you shall also have the firstling of unclean animals redeemed. Take as their redemption price, from the age of one month up, the money equivalent of five shekels by the sanctuary weight, which is twenty gerahs. (Num. 18:15–16)

A. In very ancient times, the first-born son in every Israelite family was vested with special responsibilities. From the day of his birth he was consecrated to the vocation of assisting the priest in the conduct of worship. Later, when a tabernacle was built in the wilderness, this vocation of the first-born was transferred to the Levites, a priestly tribe. The Torah then decreed that every father release his first-born son from the duties incumbent upon all first-born sons by redeeming him from a *Kohen.* The ancient obligation of the first-born son thus continues to be recalled. This practice, ordained as a recollection of the Exodus from Egypt, further serves to make vivid for us the liberation from bondage of the people of Israel, an event which has been an inspiration to all freedom loving people. *(A Rabbi's Manual,* ed. Rabbi Jules Harlow*)*

B. On the thirty-first day (postponed until evening if it falls on a Sabbath or holy day), the father presents his son symbolically to a Kohen, a descendant of a priestly family, and then receives the child back in exchange for the redemption price of five silver dollars. "The idea that the child belongs to God first and foremost is at the heart of the *pidyon ha-ben,* and this realization can be a sobering and important experience for the parents who set out to raise their first child." *(The JPS Torah Commentary: Numbers,* by Jacob Milgrom)

We have here two contemporary comments on the pidyon ha-ben. According to Rabbi Harlow, it is tied in with the Exodus. What is the connection? Milgrom quotes Gunther Plaut as relating the ceremony to the strong emotions connected with having one's first child. Perhaps some parents could share their memories of those feelings. What does it mean to say that a child belongs to God? Why particularly the first-born? Don't we feel that way about all our children?

THE TITHE TODAY

And to the Levites I hereby give all the tithes in Israel as their share in return for the services that they perform, the services of the Tent of Meeting. (18:21)

A. The amount to be given (for *tzedakah*) is as follows: If he has sufficient resources he should give according to the need of the poor; if his resources do not extend to this, he should give up to one-fifth of his possessions for an ideal fulfillment of the *mitzvah,* one-tenth for a normal fulfillment, and less corresponds to an ungenerous fulfillment. (*Shulḥan Arukh Yoreh Dei·ah* 249:1)

B. It seems definite that the tithe on money is not in the category of the mitzvah of the poor tithe, but rather that concerning the obligation to give charity, the rabbis said that it should be a tenth of one's possessions. It is a rabbinic observance coming under the law of tzedakah. (Rabbi Ḥayyim Yosef David Azulai)

C. A person must set aside 10% of his income for

tzedakah.[30] This obligation is compatible with the amount of money an average individual gives willingly to charity. . . . When calculating 10% of the salary, the net wage and not the gross wage on the salary stub is the figure to deal with. Therefore, Social Security deductions and income taxes should not be part of the final sum. Sales tax, customs and other business-related levies may also be written off as losses against the total profit. These deductible taxes may not be paid for with the separated 10% as it was sanctified for charitable use . . . Household expenses such as municipal taxes for services, health insurance payments, maid service and family food costs **may not** be deducted from the total income. They must be paid for with the remaining 90%. (*Financial Law,* by Rabbi Ezra Batzri, a contemporary summary of Jewish law relating to money)

Think about your total contributions to charity. How close do you come to this ideal? Why do you think Jewish law specified a percentage? What is the point of Rabbi Batzri's calculations to exclude taxes, Social Security, etc., and only tithe from the net wage? Why not deduct household expenses? Why not say, "Give what you can" or "Give as your heart moves you"?

QUALITY *TZEDAKAH*

You shall set aside all gifts due to the Lord from everything that is donated to you, from each thing its best portion, the part thereof that is to be consecrated. (Num. 18:29)

A. The Torah says that the tithe should be taken from the best produce, from the highest rather than lowest quality fruits and grains. . . . In other words, an effort should be made when separating the tithe that the very best, not the worst, be used.

What holds true for tithe and *terumah,* holds equally for donations to *tzedakah.* One should try to give as much as possible, but whatever amount any particular person gives, whether much or little, he should offer it with the right intent. For the penny of the man with limited means is as acceptable in the eyes of God as the dollar of the rich man. The important thing is that it should be honest money and in coin that is not damaged. This needs to be stressed, since it sometimes happens that when the charity officer goes around to collect money for buying *tallitot* and *tefillin,* or for giving to the poor, or even for providing for the sick, he often finds some of the money damaged or missing. Anyone guilty of this has not only failed to give *tzedakah,* but has actually benefited from the public purse, by depositing a worthless coin and taking in exchange two others. Moreover, if a person is sitting down to eat, and a pauper enters and he wants to give him something to eat, he should offer him the best food on the table. Accordingly, the verse stresses that *from everything that is donated to you, from each thing its best portion.* That is, whatever be the gift offered to God or for any sacred purpose, the very best and choicest should be given and not the worst. *(Yalkut Me-am Lo·ez)*

---

30. Remember that the primary use of the tithe is to help the poor. Highest priority goes to redeeming captives. Next priority is supporting the poor. It is also permitted to use the tithe for other charities, including supporting scholars, donating to synagogues, and other communal needs., including Torah and professional education of children of the poor.

It's comforting in a strange way to learn that they had similar problems in collecting tzedakah in the 18th century to those we have today. I'm not sure what the analogy would be to passing off a defective coin, but the struggle to get people to give of their best continues. What does it mean today to give of our best? What values are we expressing by requiring that the needy get the best of our funds and gifts, rather than the most meager and threadbare donations? What are we saying about the recipients? About the donors?

Parshat Ḥukkat
Numbers 19:1–22:1

1. (19:1–22) The ritual of the red heifer: An unblemished red cow is sacrificed outside the camp, and then burned down to its ashes, which were then used for ritual purification of someone who had touched a corpse.
2. (20:1–13) Moses brings water from a rock by striking it with his staff, but this contradicts God's instructions to talk to the rock, so God tells Moses and Aaron that they will not lead the people into the promised land.
3. (20:14–21) Edom refuses to allow Israel to pass through its territory, forcing them to detour.
4. (20:22–29) The death of Aaron.
5. (21:1–3) An encounter with the Canaanites.
6. (21:4–10) The people complain against God and Moses. God punishes them with poisonous snakes. After Moses intercedes, God has him set up a copper statue of a snake, which will cure anyone snake-bit who gazes upon it.
7. (21:11–20) Further stages of the Israelites' journey through the Transjordan wilderness. The Song of the Well.
8. (21:21–22:1) The conquest of the land of Sichon and Og and all of Transjordan.

HUMBLING THE HOLY

The Lord spoke to Moses and Aaron, saying: This is the law (ḥok) of the Torah that the Lord has commanded. (Num. 19:1–2)

A. *This is the law of the Torah* — It is a law enacted by God concerning this *mitzvah,* that the ashes purify the impure and make impure the pure, and you are not allowed to worry yourself about it as to why this is so. In any event, even mitzvot that have no reason, even they are full of reasons, as the Sages said, "You can make *midrashim* on them as much as the mind can endure." It is possible to say, that since it is known and revealed that the way of this world is that one who has merited to be given an exalted task, he stops being an ordinary human being, and thinks of himself as an important personage, elevated and exalted above all. Therefore the Torah said that those who are pure who are occupied with this purification of the red heifer become impure, so that they will not become arrogant in their work and feel superior to the holy people, but will be humbled, recognizing and knowing that they are but chosen messengers of the Blessed Holy One, representatives of God's people the House of Israel, and their purity is not superior to that of all of Israel. *(Min Hatorah)*

First of all, isn't it fascinating that even the passage that is the classic example of an unexplainable law of God is nevertheless given an explanation? Second, once again we find a great sensitivity to the temptations of religious leaders. In this case, the priestly functionaries are helping remove the ritual impurity which comes from contact with the dead. This was very important in the era of sacrificial worship. For example, you couldn't eat of the Paschal lamb if you were ritually impure (which is why this passage is read as a special maftir on Shabbat Parah right before Pesach). It would be easy for the priest to think that he was somehow responsible for this "magic" act of purification. Thus, the paradoxical enactment that the holy functionaries are rendered impure in the act of purification. That way, we avoid confusing the office with the person. So what would be the equivalent nowadays to keep leaders from similar errors of arrogance?

GOD HAS CONSIDERATION FOR OUR MONEY

The Presence of the Lord appeared to them, and the Lord spoke to Moses, saying, "You and your brother Aaron take the rod and assemble the community, and before their very eyes order the rock to yield its water. Thus you shall produce water for them from the rock and provide drink for the congregation and their beasts." (Num. 20:6–8)

A. Here [with the words "and their beasts"] it is hinted that the Torah has consideration for the possessions of Israel. (Talmud Tractate Menachot 76b)

B. My grandparents and their children lived across the street from a large Orthodox synagogue, of which they were members. Because of the proximity, my grandparents often hosted guests of the congregation for Shabbat. One Friday afternoon my grandmother sent my father, then a lad of fifteen or so, to ask Rabbi Solomon Scheinfeld when the guests for that week were expected. Rabbi Scheinfeld served that congregation from 1902 to 1943, and, according to the *Encyclopedia Judaica,* he "was the recognized head of the city's Orthodox congregations during his tenure." . . . When my father entered the rabbi's office, he was literally in the process of deciding whether a chicken was kosher. As Rabbi Scheinfeld turned the chicken over in his hands, he asked the woman who had brought it many questions about the physical and economic health of her husband and family. After he pronounced the chicken kosher and the woman left the room, my father asked him why he had asked so many questions about her family. The rabbi turned to my father and said, "If you think that the kosher status of chickens depends only on their physical state, you understand nothing about Jewish law!" (Elliot Dorff)

This wonderful story sums up the balance of law, justice, and morality in Judaism. Our Rabbis believed that for the law to do unwarranted harm to someone was an unacceptable result. Thus there are a number of principles that modify strict adherence to the law, of which ours here is one. Imagine that you are in a discussion with a Christian friend about religion. He raises the old charge about "the harsh God of the Old Testament and the loving God of the New Testament." How could you use this story to counter the accusation of legalism?

MOSES' SIN

Moses took the rod from before the Lord, as He had commanded him. Moses and Aaron assembled the congregation in front of the rock; and he said to them, "Listen, you rebels, shall we get water for you out of this rock?" And Moses raised his hand and struck the rock twice with his rod. Out came copious water, and the community and their beasts drank. (Num. 20:9–11)

A. At least ten explanations given by the medieval Jewish commentators deserve our serious attention. They can be subsumed under three different aspects of the biblical account:

1. Moses' action in striking the rock: (a) that he struck it instead of speaking; (b) that he chose it although the people wanted another rock; (c) that he struck it twice instead of once.
2. His character, shown by (a) his blazing temper; (b) his cowardice (in fleeing to the sanctuary, v. 6); (c) his callousness (in mourning for Miriam while his people died of thirst).
3. His words, (a) which in the form of a question were misconstrued as doubting God; (b) actually doubting God; (c) calling Israel "rebels"; (d) *notzi*, "shall *we* draw forth . . . "(Jacob Milgrom, *The JPS Torah Commentary*)

B. Rabbenu Ḥannanel writes that the sin of Moses and Aaron was that they said: (20:10) *Listen, you rebels, shall we get water for you out of this rock?* It would have been better for them to say: "Shall the Lord get water for you?" as they had said: (Exod. 16:8), *Since it is the Lord who will give you flesh to eat in the evening,* etc. Likewise at all the miracles he announced to them that God was doing them. In the present instance perhaps the people thought that Moses and Aaron drew water out of the rock by their own skill. This then was: (Deut. 32:51) *You failed to uphold My sanctity among the Israelite people.* In the first instances at Rephidim there was no opportunity for mistaking the Divine miracle: (Exod. 17:5–6) *Then the Lord said to Moses, "Pass before the people; take with you some of the elders of Israel, and take along the rod with which you struck the Nile, and set out. I will be standing there before you on the rock at Horeb. Strike the rock and water will issue from it, and the people will drink." And Moses did so in the sight of the elders of Israel.* The cloud of Divine glory hovering above the rock bore testimony to the working of a Divine miracle, whereas in the present instance no such demonstration was visible, so that they could easily have misunderstood what Moses and Aaron said *(shall we get water for you)*. It is possible that Moses and Aaron somehow took credit for it, and therefore they were indicted: (Deut. 32:51) *Because you trespassed against Me in the midst of the children of Israel at the waters of Meribah-Kadesh;* for he who benefits [improperly] from the Holy Realm is termed a *trespasser.* (Ramban)

Milgrom favors Ramban's explanation, adding, "Considering that Moses' generation had hardly been weaned from the bondage of Egypt, his error was neither slight nor pardonable." The Israelites had not yet learned to think in terms of one God. If this is the correct explanation, what does it have to say to us? We, after all, live long after the age of miracles, and paganism is not our temptation. But there are still problems with people improperly taking credit for the work of others. Have you seen this happen at work? At school? In volunteer organizations? Why is this such a pernicious form of falsehood?

WHY MOSES HAD TO REMAIN BEHIND

But the Lord said to Moses and Aaron, "Because you did not trust Me enough to affirm My sanctity in the sight of the Israelite people, therefore you shall not lead this congregation into the land that I have given them." (Num. 20:12)

A. Supposing that Moses (and through him, his people) are being taught lessons in leadership, what does denying Moses the right to enter Canaan signify?

Starting from the firmest ground, the Torah teaches that even God's chosen mediator, with whom he speaks directly, must be set limits. No man is blameless in the sense that he will not attempt, if allowed, to become more powerful than is good for himself or for others. Withholding Canaan from Moses is meant to show the necessity of limits, categories that cannot be crossed — even as limits exist in the principles of the religion Moses helped to found. That Moses constantly strives to cross over Jordan — implying he could lead the people in perpetuity, for there would always be new challenges for which they were unprepared without him — shows how much Moses, like his people, needs boundaries. Despite his subservience to the Lord, even Moses, were his power unlimited, might choose to be a god or godlike.

. . . There is no one "like unto Moses" (Deut. 34:10), the last line of Deuteronomy says, because there is not supposed to be. Why not? A new Moses would present the danger of a religion and a people permanently organized around one personality.

. . . Only the greatest leader is able to inculcate principles so profound that other people can successfully implement them well into the future. God is trying to teach Moses that the greater accomplishment is to have done this without going into Canaan . . . When Moses says that he does not get to go to Canaan because "the Lord was angry with me for your sakes," he is saying that it would not be good for the people if the leader who had taught them how to assume self-government were to deny it to them by his perpetual presence. Moses the eternal teacher would then instead be Moses the permanent master . . . It is better for the people that Moses die physically than that his character be assassinated morally.

. . . Moses eventually understands that the chief virtue in leaders is to make themselves unnecessary. To be a "nursing father" — knowing that the child may die, will probably rebel, and must be allowed to make history on his own — is the essence of Mosaic leadership. Teaching that leads to learning that creates new teachers is a circular process of renewal, not a linear model of leadership. (Aaron Wildavsky, *The Nursing Father: Moses as a Political Leader*)

Professor Wildavsky makes a number of vital and thought-provoking points here in explaining why Moses does not, and should not, get to the Promised Land. What can we learn from them that applies to issues of leadership today? Does this relate to term limits? Division of powers? What do you think of the statement that "the chief virtue in leaders is to make themselves unnecessary"? If you agree, how would you apply it to synagogues? To schools? To business corporations? If you disagree, why?

THE DEATH OF THE RIGHTEOUS

At Mount Hor, on the boundary of the land of Edom, the Lord said to Moses and Aaron, "Let Aaron be gathered to his kin: he is not to enter the land that I have assigned to the Israelite people, because you disobeyed My command about the waters of Meribah." (Num. 20:23–24)

A. *Because you disobeyed My command* — This bears on what Scripture says, *The Lord will not let the righteous go hungry* (Proverbs 10:3). It applies to Adam. All the righteous men that are to spring from him, and against whom death is decreed, will not depart this life without beholding the presence of the Shechinah, and they will reprove Adam by saying to him, "You have brought mortality upon us." Adam will answer them, "As for me, I have only one sin to my account, while in your case there is not a single person among you who has not at least four transgressions to his account!"[31] . . . The righteous are punished with death for slight transgressions. This is in order that Adam might not be called to account by them, as it says, *The Lord will not let the righteous go hungry.*[32] This is the reason why it says, *Because you disobeyed My command.* (*Midrash Numbers Rabbah* 19:18)

This text maintains that death is a part of life, a natural process which no one, not even the most righteous, escapes, yet the midrash still associates death with sin. But the matter doesn't rest there. Professor Ephraim Urbach writes in his magisterial study, The Sages: Their Concepts and Beliefs, quoting Sifre Deuteronomy, paragraph 339, "The Ministering Angels said to the Blessed Holy One, 'Sovereign of the universe, why did Adam die?' He replied, 'Because he did not fulfill My commandment.' Said they to Him, 'But Moses did fulfill Your commandments!' He answered them, 'It is My decree, the same for all humans.'" Urbach adds, "The conception of death as a decree . . . puts an end to the connection between the sin of Adam and the sins of his descendants." What difference does it make for our understanding of life if, instead of viewing death as a punishment, we accept it as a necessary part of life? Can we then make the leap to Abraham Joshua Heschel's words, "Death may be a supreme spiritual act, turning oneself over to eternity . . . Death is not sensed as a defeat but as a summation, an arrival, a conclusion"?

---

31. Not even Moses. See Exod. 4:13.
32. This is understood in the sense of "grieve." God would not allow Adam to bear the guilt of thinking that he alone was responsible for the death of the righteous. In other words, no concept of original sin, of death as a punishment. Adam has a comeback to the other righteous who accuse him of bringing death into the world: He only had the one sin, and the rest have at least four. (Soncino)

AARON THE BELOVED

When Moses and Eleazar came down from the mountain, the whole community knew that Aaron had breathed his last. All the house of Israel wept for Aaron thirty days. (Num. 20:28–29)

A. *All the house of Israel wept* — Men and women, because Aaron used to pursue peace and promote love between contending parties, and between husband and wife. (Rashi)

B. *All the house of Israel wept* — whereas for Moses only men wept, because he rendered judgment strictly according to the truth and used to rebuke people besides. But Aaron never said to a man or to a woman, "You have acted offensively." More! He sought peace, as is said, *He walked with Me in peace and uprightness* (Mal. 2:6). What is meant by the words that follow in the verse: *And did turn many away from iniquity* (ibid.)? These words teach that when Aaron would walk along the road and meet a wicked man, he greeted him warmly. The next day, when that man was about to go and commit a transgression, he would say to himself: Woe is me, how could I ever raise my eyes and face Aaron? I would be too embarrassed by the man who greeted me so warmly. The result: That wicked man would refrain from further transgression. Likewise, when two men quarreled, Aaron would go, sit with one of them, and say, "My son, look how your friend beats his breast and tears his hair out as he says, 'Woe is me, how can I raise my eyes and face my friend? I would be too embarrassed, for it is I who acted offensively toward him.'" Aaron would sit with him until he removed all rancor from his heart. Then Aaron would go and say the same thing to the other man. Later, when one met the other, they would hug and kiss each other. Hence it is said, *All the house of Israel wept.* (Avot D'Rabbi Natan 12; Yalkut Shimoni, Hukkat, #764)

This is such a rich midrash! It raises many issues for discussion. 1) The people loved Aaron more than they loved Moses, yet Moses is the one more remembered by future generations. What was it about Aaron that they loved? What was it about Moses that they found less lovable? Could Aaron have been "Rabbenu," our teacher and leader? 2) Aaron never rebuked anyone. Instead, he had another method for turning people to the right path. Why and how was this effective? Does it provide any model for us today? 3) Aaron lied in order to make peace between quarrelers. Was that justified?

LOVING ARGUMENT

For the Arnon is the boundary of Moab, between Moab and the Amorites. Therefore the Book of the Wars of the Lord speaks of " . . . Vahev in Suphah, and the wadis: the Arnon, with its tributary wadis, stretched along the settled country of Ar, hugging the territory of Moab . . . " (Num. 21:13–15)

A. It is also said: *Happy is the man who fills his quiver with them, they shall not be put to shame when they contend with the enemy in the gate* (Psalm 127:5).[33] What is meant by *with the enemy in the gate*? — Said R. Ḥiyya b. Abba: Even father and son, master and disciple, who study Torah at the same gate[34] become enemies of each other;[35] yet they do not stir from there until they come to love each other, for it is written, *therefore the Book of the Wars of the Lord speaks of* love[36] as *be-sufah* (in Sufah); read not *'be-sufah'* but *'be-sofah'* (at the end).[37] (Talmud Tractate Kiddushin 30b)

Admittedly, this text strays far from the contextual meaning of the verse. However, that's one of the pleasures of rabbinic commentary. As someone taught me at seminary, there are texts, and pretexts! Whenever we come across the expression, "read not x but y," we know that the Rabbis are engaged in word play, in this case a change in vocalization. In this case, their playing field is place names, the type of verse we would not usually think to interpret beyond trying to identify the location. However, for our Rabbis, the Torah has many layers of meaning to be explored. The result here is a lovely teaching about intellectual "combat" and collegiality. In the heat of discussion, tempers can rise, but arguments about Torah must be resolved lovingly, or something is seriously wrong. Someone once said that the reason that academic politics are so fierce is that there is so little at stake! In Torah arguments, there is much at stake — discovering the meaning(s) of the word of God, applying them to daily life in the covenant community — but also the relationships of the disputants. In order for us to know that the arguments are for the sake of discerning truth, they must end in love. How, then, can we apply this rule of loving argument to our lives today? Let's look at another set of concentric circles: our family, our synagogue, the Jewish community, the general community, American politics.

THE MITZVAH OF MAKING PEACE

Israel sent messengers to Sihon, king of the Amorites, saying, "Let me pass through your country. We will follow the king's highway until we have crossed your territory." But Sihon would not let Israel pass through his territory. (Num. 21:21–23)

A. *Israel sent messengers* — Now the Torah did not insist that we should go in pursuit of the commandments, but said: *If a bird's nest chances to be before you . . .* (Deut. 22:6); *If you meet the ox of your neighbor* (Exod. 23:4); *When you gather the grapes of your vineyard* (Deut. 24:20). . . In all these cases, if they come your way you are commanded to perform the duties connected with them, but you need not go in pursuit of them. In the case of peace, however, *seek peace,*

33. The preceding verse reads: *Like arrows in the hand of a warrior are sons born to a man in his youth.* On which Rashi comments, "A person's students are called his children."
34. Note in the Soncino translation: "I.e., at the same academy. Alternatively, in the same subject."
35. Rashi says, "Because they argue with each other, and this one does not accept the words of the other.
36. *Vahev,* connected by a play on words with *ahav,* to love.
37. Rashi explains "The Book of the Wars" — a war that is by means of a book will end up with love. Soncino: "The book of the wars of the Lord" — i.e., disputations on Biblical interpretation — eventually lead to love.

wherever you happen to be, *and pursue it* (Ps. 34:15) if it is elsewhere. Israel in fact acted this way. Although the Blessed Holy One had said: *Begin the occupation: engage him in battle* (Deut. 2:24), they pursued peace, *And Israel sent messengers to Sihon . . . Let me pass through your country.* (*Midrash Numbers Rabbah* 19:27)

B. No war is to be waged with anyone in the world before offering terms of peace, whether it is an optional or an obligatory war, as it is written: *When you approach a town to attack it, you shall offer it terms of peace* (Deut. 20:10). . . . When a city is besieged in order to capture it, it must not be surrounded on all four sides but only on three sides, so as to leave room for flight for whoever wishes to flee for his life. (Maimonides, *Mishneh Torah,* Laws of Kings 6:1, 7)

How did Moses dare to disobey God's order? Why didn't God mind? On the basis of the laws quoted here, what modern tactics of warfare would Jewish law condemn? Note that Maimonides includes even an obligatory war — one fought in self-defense or for the conquest of the Land of Israel — in the imperative to offer peaceful terms. What can we learn from this about the importance of peace-making?

WHO DESERVES THE GIFT OF LEARNING?

And from Midbar to Mattanah [In Hebrew, umi-midbar mattanah, literally: "and from the wilderness, a gift."], and from Mattanah to Nachaliel, and from Nachaliel to Bamot, and from Bamot to the valley (Num. 21:18)

A. Rava said: If one makes himself as a wilderness, open to all, then the Torah is given to him as a gift *(mattanah),* as it is written, *And from the desert, mattanah.* And once it is given to him as a gift, the Lord causes him to inherit it, as it is written, *and from Mattanah, Nachaliel* ["the inheritance of the Lord"]. And once he inherits it, he ascends to greatness, as it is written: *and from Nachaliel, Bamot* ["the high place"]. But if he exalts *himself,* the Blessed Holy One brings him low, as it is written, *and from Bamot to the valley.* And not that alone, but he even sinks into the ground, as it is written: *overlooking the wasteland.* (Talmud Tractate Nedarim 55b)

First we must understand what it means to be "open to all." The Hebrew word is hefker, which means "ownerless, in the public domain." So what does it mean for an individual to be hefker? One understanding is that the scholar should both learn and teach with humility. This fits well with the injunction to the scholar not to exalt himself. Why is the humble, accessible scholar rewarded with greater learning, while the one who exalts himself is brought low? Do you think this is a threat of Divine punishment, or a factual description of what happens to people?

PERSPECTIVE

Now Cheshbon was the city of Sichon king of the Amorites, who had fought against a former king of Moab and taken all his land from him as far as the Arnon. Therefore the bards [hamoshelim] would recite: "Come to Cheshbon; firmly built and well founded is Sichon's city." (Num. 21:26–27)

A. R. Samuel said in the name of R. Yochanan: What is the meaning of the verse, Therefore *hamoshelim* would recite? — *Hamoshelim* means those who rule their evil inclinations. Come to *Cheshbon*, means, come, let us consider the account of the world; the loss incurred by the fulfillment of a mitzvah against the reward incurred by its observance, and the gain gotten by a transgression against the loss it involves. *Firmly built and well founded* — if you do so, you shall be built in this world and you shall be well founded in the world to come. (Talmud Baba Batra 78b)

This is an example of a symbolic interpretation of a verse, involving a lot of word-play. Moshelim here means "reciters of parables, bards" but the root [mem-shin-lamed] can also mean, "rulers." Cheshbon is a place name, but the Hebrew word can also mean "reckon, account for." So read it, "You who would rule over your evil inclination, take an account of your deeds (consider the ultimate result, for sometimes doing wrong gives a short-term gain, whereas doing the right thing involves a short-term loss), and if you do so you will stand firm both in this world and the next." In other words, the first step toward living an ethical life is self-awareness and consciousness of the impact of our deeds, includingh taking a long-term view. What interferes with this awareness? How can we gain this perspective? How can friends help each other get this perspective?

Parshat Balak
Numbers 22:2–25:9

1. (22:2–7) Balak, King of Moab, invites Balaam, who has the power to bless and curse, to help him by cursing the Israelites.
2. (22:8–20) Balak's messengers deliver his proposal to Balaam, who tells them he must consult with God before he can decide. God first tells him not to go. Balak sends a second delegation, whom Balaam also refuses. God tells Balaam that he may go, *but whatever I command you, that shall you do.*
3. (22:21–38) Balaam sets out riding his donkey. On the way, an angel of the Lord appears. He does not see it, but his donkey does, and refuses to move. Balaam beats it to force it to go on. After being beaten three times, the donkey speaks, complaining of this ill treatment. God then opens Balaam's eyes so that he sees the angel, who also rebukes Balaam for beating the donkey. Balaam offers to turn back. The angel tells him to go, but warns him again only to say what God tells him. Balak meets Balaam at the border, and tells him that he *can only utter the word that God puts into my mouth.*
4. (22:39–41) Balaam arrives in Moab and is received by Balak with great honor.
5. (23:1–26) To Balak's distress, Balaam, compelled by God, blesses and praises the Israelites, and predicts great things for their future. This happens twice.
6. (23:27–24:9) Balaam makes a third attempt. In this blessing, he says the well-known words of the Mah Tovu, *How lovely are your tents, O Jacob, your dwellings, O Israel!* He concludes, *Blessed are they who bless you, accursed those who curse you!*
7. (24:10–19) Balak, totally infuriated, tells Balaam that he won't pay him, and discharges him. Balaam reminds him that he said all along that he could only say what God told him to say, and throws in a fourth blessing, unsolicited, predicting Israel's conquest of Moab.
8. (24:20–25) Balaam goes on to make predictions concerning other nations.
9. (25:1–9) The incident at Baal Peor, where Moabite women entice Israelite men into sexual promiscuity and idolatry. Pinḥas, Aaron's grandson, sees one Israelite man brazenly bring a Midianite woman to his tent in front of the whole community. He kills them both, averting a plague.

CAUSELESS HATRED (SIN·AT ḤINAM)

[Balak to Balaam] Come then, put a curse upon this people for me, since they are too numerous for me; perhaps I can thus defeat them and drive them out of the land. For I know that he whom you bless is blessed indeed, and he whom you curse is cursed. (Num. 22:6)

A. Since Balak knew that *he whom you bless is blessed indeed,* why did he hire Balaam to curse Israel. Wouldn't it have been better for him to hire Balaam to bless Moab so that it would be victorious in war? This is proof that the essential intention of the enemies of Israel is not to benefit their own people, but to do evil to Israel, and all their rage against Israel is not a result of their love of their own people, but out of hatred for Israel. As a result of this great hatred they spoil everything and bring a curse upon their people and their land. *(Itturei Torah)*

B. The first Temple was destroyed because of idolatry, immorality and murder, but the second Temple was destroyed because of causeless hatred *(sin·at ḥinam).* This teaches us that causeless hatred is a sin that weighs as heavily as idolatry, immorality and murder. (Talmud Yoma 9b)

This is a strong teaching about the power of hatred. It makes us think of the Nazis persisting with their genocidal project even at the cost of their war effort, or the Palestinians harming their own interests out of their hatred for Israel. Why does hatred have this power? Why is it sometimes more satisfying to see our enemies suffer than to enjoy our own well-being (the opposite of "living well is the best revenge")? In order to understand the second comment properly, know that idolatry, sexual immorality, and bloodshed were the three sins that, rather than be forced to violate them, one would rather die. In short, they are the three most serious sins. How do we overcome hatred? The Ḥafetz Ḥayyim suggests that this is the reason the Torah extends the law of ḥesed, of doing kind deeds, to enemies: "If you meet your enemy's ox or his donkey going astray, you shall surely bring it back to him again" (Exod. 23:4). Furthermore, "If the one against whom he harbors an unjustified hatred and a friend both requested the same favor, and he is unable to help both, he is duty bound to help the one he hates, so as to overcome his prejudices." What is the Ḥafetz Ḥayyim's method? Do you think it would work? Why doesn't he worry about "who started it?" or whether the other person deserves our help? How do we benefit when we learn to let go of hatred?

GOLDEN HANDCUFFS

Balaam replied to Balak's officials, "Though Balak were to give me his house full of silver and gold, I could not do anything, big or little, contrary to the command of the Lord my God." (Num. 22:18)

A. *Though Balak were to give me his house full of silver and gold* — This tells us that he was greedy and coveted other people's wealth. He thought: It is appropriate for him to give me all his gold and silver, for he would have to hire many soldiers, with the outcome doubtful whether he would win or lose, and I would certainly win. (Rashi)

Rashi here represents one tradition about why Balaam, who represented himself as a believer in God, and who had been warned by God not to curse Israel, still went ahead: greed. This is based on the sound psychological insight that it was Balaam who brought up large sums of money, not Balak! Balaam was willing to sacrifice his principles for the sake of wealth. To what extent is this necessary in today's world? We hear about people having "golden handcuffs," salaries and perquisites that bind them to jobs they find morally distasteful, or that force them to work long hours and neglect their families. Are they really trapped? How can one break free from golden handcuffs?

THE SCANDAL OF THE SUPERNATURAL

Then the Lord opened the donkey's mouth, and she said to Balaam, "What have I done to you that you have beaten me these three times?" (Num. 22:28)

A. Ten things were created on the eve of the sabbath at twilight,[38] and these are they: [1] the mouth of the earth,[39] [2] the mouth of the well,[40] [3] the mouth of the she-donkey, [4] the rainbow,[41] [5] the manna, [6] the rod [of Moses], [7] the shamir,[42] [8] the text,[43] [9] the writing,[44] and [10] the tablets.[45] (*Pirkei Avot* 5:6)

B. From the very beginning of Creation, God included in the nature of every created thing whatever He was going to do with it — whether it would always behave uniformly and hence in accordance with the laws of nature, or act extraordinarily, that is, be a miracle. (Maimonides, *Commentary on the Mishnah*)

C. The concept of the Fathers, the authors of *Abot*, was that the supernatural incidents, or miracles, enumerated in this Mishnah, were really not supernatural. They were special creations made by God at the creation, which were to take place at the time needed in the future, and are therefore a part of the natural course of events. (Hyman E. Goldin)

These comments are based on the opinion that there is something scandalous and disturbing about miracles. One of the reassuring consequences of believing in one God who rules over nature, rather than many gods who personify forces of nature, is that there is dependable and consistent natural law. Start making exceptions to that, and you reintroduce an element of

38. Between the sixth day of creation and the seventh, when God rested.
39. That swallowed up Korah and his company.
40. According to the midrash, a well followed the Israelites around in the wilderness to provide them with water. This was attributed to Miriam's merit.
41. Of Noah's Flood.
42. A legendary worm or insect which by passing over stones could make an incision for an engraving or split them through completely. Such an assumption was deemed necessary in view of the command that no iron tool be lifted at the building of an altar to God and, of the report in I Kings 6:7, that in fact no such tool was heard during the building of Solomon's Temple.
43. The letters of the Decalogue
44. The words formed by the letters, or, according to others, the writing instrument used to form the letters.
45. All three were unique. "They were the expression in God's own language, in God's own script, on God's own instrument, of the messages that were vital for the society to be created by the people of Israel." (Rabbi Reuven Bulka)

uncertainty and caprice. So the solution is to consider the miracles to be built in exceptions (subroutines?) to the normal order of nature. Many modern believers have their own problems with believing in miracles. Does the approach presented here help?

WHO IS THE DONKEY HERE?

Then the Lord opened the donkey's mouth, and she said to Balaam, "What have I done to you that you have beaten me these three times?" (Num. 22:28)

A. *Then the Lord opened the donkey's mouth* — That is, he gave the donkey the power of speech. These words are a satiric play on Balaam's reputed prophetic gifts, for the Lord also uses Balaam's mouth as the vehicle for His message. (Jacob Milgrom, *The JPS Torah Commentary*)

B. This was to bring it home forcibly to Balaam that he had no cause to consider himself great because he had been endowed with prophetic vision. Why, even the donkey, which certainly would not be considered fit to look upon an angel, or to speak, was enabled to do both because it was for the good of the Children of Israel. Balaam was no more fit to be a prophet than the donkey, and was given the gift of prophecy only in order that the Children of Israel might benefit thereby. *(K'li Yakar)*

C. The other nations had heard that Moses' power was derived from his mouth, and didn't realize that this meant his prayer, and instead thought that it referred to his great powers of oratory. They therefore went and hired Balaam who was also a great speaker, and had exceptional powers of cursing people, in order to overpower Moses' strength. Therefore, *the Lord opened the donkey's mouth,* God showed them that a donkey too can be a great orator. *(Imray Kohen)*

These comments all point out that there is a strong satirical element in the Balaam narrative. The greatest prophet and sage of the gentiles is bested in spiritual vision, moral sensitivity, obedience to God and oratorical ability by a donkey! What do you think these humorous comments teach us?

A PEOPLE THAT DWELLS APART

As I see them from the mountain tops
Gaze on them from the heights,/
There is a people that dwells apart,
Not reckoned among the nations. (Num. 23:9)

A. Often it seems that the special task of Judaism is to express the idea of *the people that dwells apart,* the ethical principle of the minority. Judaism bears witness to the power of the idea as against the power of mere numbers and worldly success; it stands for the enduring protest of those who seek to be true to their own selves, who assert their right to be different against the crushing pressure of the vicious and the leveling. This too is a way of constant preaching to the world.

By its mere existence Judaism is a never silent protest against the assumption of the multitude that force is superior to truth. So long as Judaism exists, nobody will be able to say that the soul of humanity has surrendered. Its very existence through the ages is proof that conviction cannot be mastered by numbers . . . (Leo Baeck, *The Essence of Judaism*)

Baeck emphasizes the religious and ethical courage required to be a Jew. Jewish identity has "been developed through the lives of those who in the name of their God always had the will to live in opposition to the many, and who, in order not to become estranged from Him, endured estrangement upon earth." Is this still true? In order to be a Jew, to live a Jewish life, does one have to "dwell apart" to some significant degree? How do Shabbat and Kashrut relate to the idea of dwelling apart? Is this kind of psychological strength more necessary in order to be a practicing Jew in Diaspora? How about the State of Israel? Does it seem at times that it, too, fulfills this notion of "dwelling apart"?

BALAAM'S CHARACTER

A. Whoever possesses these three qualities is numbered among the disciples of our ancestor Abraham, and those who possess the three opposite qualities are found among the disciples of wicked Balaam: A generous spirit, a humble soul, a modest appetite — such a one is a disciple of our ancestor Abraham; A grudging spirit, an arrogant soul, an insatiable appetite — such a one is a disciple of wicked Balaam. (*Pirkei Avot* 5:21)

B. **A grudging spirit** (*ayin ra'a,* literally, an evil eye) — Jealousy: Whatever belongs to him seems little, and what belongs to his neighbor seems much. (Yosef Yavetz) Before Israel went out of Egypt, all the nations in the world used to consult Balaam; after Israel went out of Egypt, even a maidservant in Israel was wiser than he. He began therefore to be jealous of Israel. (Avot of Rabbi Nathan B)

An arrogant soul (*ru'ach g'vohah,* literally: a high spirit) — Note the verse, *For the Lord will not let me go with you* (Num. 22:13) — That is to say, shall I go with the likes of you? I will go only with those greater than you! And the end of the matter was that, *Then Balak sent other dignitaries, more numerous and distinguished than the first* (22:15). (Avot of Rabbi Nathan B)

An insatiable appetite (*nefesh r'ḥavah,* literally, a wide soul) — Because it is written, *If Balak would give me his house full of silver and gold* (22:18). "If," he told them, "Balak desired to hire for himself armies to fight against them, he would be in doubt as to whether they would be victorious or whether they would fall. Is it not worth his while that he should give me all that wealth and be sure of victory?" Thus you learn that he actually asked for this. (Midrash Numbers Rabbah 20:10)

C. As for the disciples of Balaam, their malice, their arrogance, and their insatiable greed and ambition not only make it impossible for them to walk upon the road to salvation in the world to come, but also keep them from finding one moment's true contentment, even in the midst of an abundance of riches and pleasures. Any joy, honor, or prosperity that comes to others is a bitter drop in their cup of joy and whatever they may already have achieved loses all value in their eyes when they contemplate those of their desires that are still unfulfilled. (Samson Raphael Hirsch)

What do all these negative traits have in common? An unrelenting egotism and self-centeredness. Balaam represents the "win-lose" mentality: In order for me to feel like a winner, someone else must lose. I must always be on top. The one who dies with the most toys wins. Abraham, symbolizing Jewish values, represents the opposite character: able to rejoice at others' good fortune, humble, in control of his appetites and desires. In our current culture, who would be more likely to win fame and acclaim, an Abraham or a Balaam? What aspects of contemporary culture foster the Balaam mentality? What can we do to acquire these Jewish traits of generosity, humility, and contentment?

MAH TOVU — THE BLESSING

How lovely are your tents, O Jacob, your dwellings, O Israel! (Num. 24:5)

A. The Siddur of R. Amram Gaon[46] already takes it for granted that certain verses should be recited upon the worshipper's entry into the synagogue, that he should say: *How lovely are your tents . . .* Objections were raised to the recital of this verse. R. Abraham Berliner observes that "R. Solomon Luria vehemently protested against its recital, in his responsa, since it was originally uttered by Balaam, an idolater. The Talmud, however, regards the verse as applying to synagogues and houses of Torah study." (B. S. Jacobson, *The Weekday Siddur*)

B. "Your tents" refers to your synagogues and places of study. They are indeed lovely and splendid from outside, but it is not the external beauty that is determinative. The essential is "your dwellings," what dwells within these buildings. Internal beauty is of the essence. *(Otzar Ḥayyim)*

Balaam first said Mah Tovu in response to the sight of the Israelite camp spread out before him. Rabbinic interpretation applied it to our synagogues and schools. But what makes these places holy? What makes them the true heirs of the Temple? The second comment gives us some ideas. What can we do to create that internal beauty in our own synagogues?

MAH TOVU — THE CURSE

A. What is the difference between a true and a false prophet? True prophets are rebukers. They point out defects and deficiencies and they want to change the status quo. False prophets praise the people with sweet talk, and don't see any problems. All is well, and there is nothing to correct. But the true prophets, the reprovers, are the ones who truly love the people. It was not out of great love for Israel that Balaam sang so many songs and praises to them. On the contrary, he intended to persuade them that they didn't have to do anything, that they didn't need to aspire to ascend the ladder of merit. They were perfect, blessed with all good qualities. That is the difference between him and true prophets of Israel. (Toldot Ya'akov Yosef)

46. Rav Amram Gaon was Gaon (head) of the Sura Yeshiva in Babylonia, one of the major centers of Jewish learning in his time, the 10th century. In response to a question from Spain (the other end of the Jewish world of that time), he set out the order of worship. His answer became the first authoritative edition of the Siddur.

This clever comment suggests that a good friend, family member, or leader is able to give a loving rebuke. Someone once said, "Is it possible for a man to make a fool of himself in public and not know about it? — Not if he has a wife!" How can we give and accept such loving criticism in our personal and organizational lives? (Hint: It isn't easy!) What about our political system? The American public has been accused of voting only for candidates who tell us all is well and no sacrifices are required, that we want to be lied to. How does that fit with this comment about Balaam the flatterer? *This may originally have been intended as mockery, but actually, whether a spouse, partner, or good friend, we all need someone to give us perspective on ourselves.*

TORAH AND POVERTY

Water shall flow from His pails,
***Their roots have abundant water.** (Num. 24:7)*

A. They [scholars in the Land of Israel] sent word from there: . . . Be heedful [not to neglect] the children of the poor, for from them Torah goes forth, as it is written, *Water shall flow from His pails (mi-dalyav)*: [meaning] from the *dal-lim* [poor] amongst them goes forth Torah. (Nedarim 81a)

B. Furthermore, one can explain this as meaning that the children of the rich are caught up in pleasures and indulgences, and it is the nature of Torah to be sustained by a limited way of life, as it says in Chapter 6 of Pirkei Avot, "Such is the way [of life conducive to the study] of the Torah: A morsel of bread with salt shall you eat, and water by measure shall you drink, and upon the ground shall you sleep, and a life of privation shall you live, and in the Torah shall you labor." The essence of this interpretation is the association of water with Torah, as it says in the Talmud (Tractate Babba Kamma 82a), "There is no water other than Torah." *(Torah Temimah)*

C. This does not mean that a wealthy person should reduce himself to a life of penury, but that even if a person is so poor that he can afford no more than bread with salt, etc., study of the law is nevertheless expected of him; if one is rich, his duty to engage in the study of the Torah is all the greater. (Rashi)

Given that the North American Jewish community is the wealthiest in our history, the discussion between these texts is definitely challenging. Is it true that the pursuit of wealth is incompatible with a life of Torah? We usually like to boast that Judaism doesn't demand an ascetic style of life from us — no vows of poverty, celibacy, and so on — but is that only comparatively true? Does there come a point when we should decide that we have enough, and adjust our life priorities to make more room for Torah study and Jewish practice? And what about Rashi's comment?

IGNORING LIFE'S LESSONS

***Then Balaam set out on his journey back home; and Balak also went his way.** (Num. 24:25)*

A. What does this teach us, and what difference does it make that they returned to their places? Rather the verse comes to show us how wicked they were: even though Balaam had seen by means of prophecy how great Israel were and Balak had heard all this, the two nevertheless went back to their ways — their evil ways as at the beginning — and did not learn a lesson. *(Korban ha-Ani)*

The problem that prompts this comment is that this seems like a totally superfluous verse. Of course they went home! But the Torah wants to teach us something deeper: that they went home unchanged. I recently heard someone comment, "We usually say that a wise person learns from his mistakes. Not so! That's a dumb person. A wise person learns from someone else's mistakes!" And, in fact, some of what the Torah teaches is other people's mistakes: Jacob's trickiness, young Joseph's impetuosity, Moses' temper. Here we have Balaam and Balak modeling behavior worse than foolish — they are oblivious to their own experience. So what can we learn from them and how can we apply it? We learn how hard it really is to learn from our life experience and to use it for positive change. Maybe that's why every day, three times a day, the Amidah has a prayer for repentance. Maybe that's one hint at how we can build in the capacity to learn and grow. How can we structure our lives so that we are not doomed to repeat the same counterproductive behaviors?

Parshat Pinḥas
Numbers 25:10–30:1

1. (25:7–15) Pinḥas is rewarded for his quick action, killing an Israelite who was consorting with a Midianite woman and worshipping Baal. He will be the High Priest and his descendants after him.
2. (25:16–18) The Midianites are condemned as enemies of the Jewish people.
3. (26:1–51) The second census, prior to occupying the promised land.
4. (26:52–57) God tells Moses how the land will be distributed: The location of the tribe's territory will be determined by drawing lots, but the size of the territory will be according to the size of the tribe.
5. (26:57–65) The Levite clans, listed separately because they did not get any portion of the land.
6. (27:1–11) The daughters of Zelophehad want to inherit his portion of the land, for he left no sons. God agrees that they may inherit.
7. (27:12–23) Joshua is appointed to succeed Moses as leader of the people after Moses' death.
8. (28:1–8) The daily sacrifices offered on behalf of the community.
9. (28:9–10) The additional *(musaf)* sacrifices offered on Shabbat.
10. (28:11–15) The additional sacrifices offered on Rosh Chodesh.
11. 1(28:16–30:1) The additional sacrifices offered on Passover, Shavuot, Rosh Hashanah, Yom Kippur, and Sukkot. This part of the Book of Numbers details the special sacrifices for various holy days. This section provides the maftir readings for all the festivals, and passages from it are also included in the Musaf Amidah, which takes its name from the Musaf sacrifices.

REAR-GUARD GENERALS

A. What does the juxtaposition of the Torah portions Balak and Pinḥas teach us? Balak son of Tzippor, King of Moab, was full of terror and fear of the Israelites: *"There is a people that came out of Egypt; it hides the earth from view, and it is settled next to me"* (Num. 22:5).

What was his response? What was his military effort? He sent messengers to hire Balaam: *Come then, put a curse upon this people for me* (Num. 22:6).

He himself was caught up in his merry-making, his luxuries and his pleasures, and he was too lazy even to open his impure mouth and utter a curse.

That was not the case with Pinḥas, one of the zealous priests, but rather, *When Pinḥas . . . saw this,* immediately, *he took a spear in his hand.* He didn't delay and wait for his work to be done by others. In a place where there were no men, he tried to be a man of war, saying and doing, speaking and fulfilling. *(Al Hatorah)*

The last sentence is a reference to Hillel's saying, "Where there are no men, strive to be a man." The translation in Siddur Sim Shalom renders it, "Where there are no worthy persons, strive to be a worthy person." Our text understands Pinḥas's action as a leadership function. Moses and the other onlookers did not act, and so Pinḥas stepped in. How can we apply this lesson to contemporary issues of leadership in Congress, in the presidency, and in the executive suites of business?

BE WARY OF ZEALOTRY

The Pinḥas episode is a good example of how ethics and worldview change. The Torah considers Pinḥas to be a hero. But as early as the Rabbinic period, there is discomfort with his zealous act. I have included a larger number of texts here because the point about zealotry seems to need constant emphasis.

A. The two Torah portions preceding *Pinḥas,* namely *Ḥukkat* and *Balak,* are in most cases read together on one Shabbat, and the same is true for the two following it, *Mattot* and *Masei.* On the other hand, *Parashat Pinḥas* is always read by itself. The reason is because Pinḥas was a zealot, and every zealot is on his own. Woe to the generation whose zealots unite. (Rabbi Yisrael Eiger)

B. Apparently this isn't the beginning of this Torah portion but really the end of the previous portion, the first telling of Pinḥas's deed and the second dealing with his reward. So why are the two passages separated? What is the reason for the separation? Say as follows: that one does not hurry to reward zealotry. If you are zealous, wait a bit until you have first examined your deeds very well, to make sure that they are entirely and solely for the sake of Heaven, without any hint of self-interest or personal motives. (Rabbi Moses of Kotzi)

C. If one cohabits with an Aramite woman, the zealous strike him. It was taught: But the Sages do not look with favor upon this. Now was Pinḥas regarded unfavorably by the Sages? R. Yuda ben Pazzi said: They were ready to excommunicate him had the Holy Spirit not "sprung forward" and said: *It shall be for him and his descendants after him a pact of priesthood for all time* (Num. 25:13). (Jerusalem Talmud Tractate Sanhedrin 9:7)

D. How the commentators have labored to interpret this derashah, but in truth it can be explained simply, that when it says that he acted without the approval of the Sages, it means that the Sages were not comfortable with zealots attacking someone who cohabits with an Aramite woman. One can explain it thus: that since this must be done with a true spirit of zeal for the honor of God, it is impossible to give general permission to everyone to attack a person like this. For who knows, perhaps he does this out of some selfish motive and says that he does it with the spirit of zeal for God, and ends up killing someone who is not liable to the death penalty by law . . . That is why the Sages wished to excommunicate Pinḥas, had not the Holy Spirit testified that his zeal for God was genuine. *(Torah Temimah)*

E. R. Hisda said: If the zealot comes to take counsel [whether to punish the transgressors enumerated in the Mishnah], we do not instruct him to do so. It has been stated likewise: Rabbah ben Bar Hana said in R. Johanan's name: If he comes to take counsel, we do not instruct him to do so. What is more, had Zimri forsaken his mistress and Pinḥas slain him, Pinḥas would have been executed on his account [for the zealot may slay only when the offender is engaged in the commission of the offence]; and had Zimri turned upon Pinḥas and slain him, he would not have been executed, since Pinḥas was a pursuer [seeking to take his life]. (Talmud Tractate Sanhedrin 82a)

F. "Rav Naḥman said, 'The *vav* in *shalom* is broken off'" (Kiddushin 66b). That is to say, it is written *shalim* instead of *shalom*, to teach us that zeal is a trait and not a trait. I.e., in and of itself it is not a proper trait, and it can only be justified in certain limited cases. Even the most exalted purpose is not valid to sanctify the means. There doesn't seem to a way to say this too often! Go and learn, you have no zeal like the zeal of Pinḥas [in its purity and lack of base motives]. This is why God approved of it. And even so the *shalom* that flowed from him was broken. *(Otzar Ḥayyim)*

G. Beware of intolerance, and beware of tolerance for the intolerant. There is a fine line that separates passion from violence and zeal from zealotry. Beware of the tendency to deny that any other position can have merit, that your concern takes precedence over every other consideration, that the adversary is invariably demonized, that every means is legitimate to achieve your end. Those who passionately take strong positions in Jewish life must know that there are unbalanced people who flock to extremes and who can, with what they consider good intentions, subvert the noblest goals. You who are wise, be careful with your words. (Norman Lamm)

Since these texts expressing the general wariness and caution of later tradition about Pinḥas were compiled over a decade ago, it seems that religious and political zealotry have become even more prevalent. On the one hand, the Torah clearly approves of his action; on the other, it sets a terrible precedent. That is why all of these comments do their best to say that it is no precedent at all. The Jewish tradition would agree with Jonathan Swift: "Violent zeal for truth hath an hundred to one odds to be either petulancy, ambition, or pride." Yigal Amir, Rabin's assassin, is an obvious example of the dangers of zealotry, so let's go beyond him and talk about other examples of this affliction, even those in our own hearts. Think about how Judaism uses the boundaries of law and ethics to prevent excesses of religious fervor.

FORGIVENESS IS ALWAYS POSSIBLE

The sons of Korah, however, did not die. (Num. 26:11)

A. The Korahite clan survived to become an important Levitical clan of Temple singers. Their name appears in the titles of Psalms 42, 44–49, 84, 85, and 87, and as Temple guards in 1 Chronicles 9:19. (Jacob Milgrom, *The JPS Torah Commentary*)

B. *The sons of Korah, however, did not die* — What was the merit of the sons of Korah that they were rescued? When they sat with Korah their father and saw Moses approaching, they hid their heads in shame, and said, if we stand up before Moses, we will treat our father with contempt, but if we don't stand up, it is already written in the Torah, *You shall rise before the aged* (Lev. 19:32). It is better for us to stand before Moses our teacher, even though we will thereby show disrespect for our father. At that very moment they repented in their hearts. (*Yalkut Shim·oni* 752)

C. The verse *My heart overflows with a goodly matter* (Ps. 45:2)[47] is meant to teach you that even when people are unable to confess with their mouths but their hearts are overflowing with repentance, the Blessed Holy One receives them. Indeed, the sons of Korah could not utter a song with their mouths before the Blessed Holy One, but when their hearts overflowed with repentance, God immediately received them. And why could not the sons of Korah utter a song? Because the pit was open before them and a fire burned about them . . . *My heart overflows with a goodly matter; I utter my songs to the King.* But if the heart overflows, what need for speech? And if speech were enough, why should the overflowing heart be mentioned? This is what the sons of Korah said, however: If our hearts overflow, it is the same as uttering our songs to God. Hence they said: *I utter my songs to the king* [even though the heat of the fire prevented them from opening their mouths, and so God rescued them]. (*Midrash Tehillim* 45:2)

Korah is one of the greatest villains in the Torah, yet his sons and their descendants are honored. Why? Because they repented. From this we learn that Judaism rejects guilt by association and inherited guilt. We also learn that each individual stands before God on his or her own merit. Think for a moment about Korah's sons' dilemma as described in Yalkut Shim·oni: which to follow, respect for a parent, or respect for an honored teacher and leader? This raises the question: What if your parent is not deserving of honor? What if he or she is dishonest, or abusive? Midrash Tehillim gives us a picture of how anxious God is to forgive the repentant. One doesn't have to speak a word, just repent in one's heart. God will take it from there. This prompts us to think about the other side of repentance: forgiveness. How willing to forgive are we? How far are we willing to extend ourselves? If the offender is a parent or other family member, in what ways is it appropriate to seek reconciliation?

47. One of the Psalms attributed to the sons of Korah.

WHEN THE LAW IS UNFAIR

The daughters of Zelophehad, of Manassite family . . . came forward, . . . and they said, "Our father died in the wilderness. . . . and he has left no sons. Let not our father's name be lost to his clan just because he had no son! Give us a holding among our father's kinsmen!" (Num. 27:1–4)

A. When the daughters of Zelophehad heard that the land was being divided by tribes and that daughters were not included, they gathered together to take counsel, and they said: Not as the mercies of flesh and blood are those of the Blessed Holy One. The mercies of flesh and blood are greater for males than for females, but the mercies of the Blessed Holy One are [equal] for all, as it is written (Ps. 145:9): *His mercy is upon all His works. (Sifrei)*

B. [Elsewhere in the ancient Near East, daughters could inherit.] How then are we to explain the fact that the Bible gives women no inheritance rights except in the case where there are no sons? And in that situation, unmarried daughters inherit for the purpose of transferring the estate to his grandsons! The differences in the law must reflect a difference in the makeup of the respective societies. [The Bible, based on a tightly knit clan structure, wants to prevent land being transferred to the daughter's husband's clan. Israel's neighbors were already centralized urban societies with no such clan concerns.]

. . . What happened in postbiblical times, when the clan structure of Israel had completely disintegrated? There would then have been no logical reason for maintaining laws, such as those of inheritance, whose main purpose (to perpetuate the clan) was no longer relevant. But relevant or not, the law had become canon, a divine command that had to be strictly obeyed. Thus, when the rabbis flesh out the law of inheritance to cover cases unanticipated by the biblical law they have no choice but to apply the agnatic[48] principle . . . Inheritance passes through the male line. No wonder that this inequity bothered the rabbis throughout the ages; indeed, they took great pains to compensate the daughter for the deprivation in matters of inheritance. The early tannaitic[49] rabbis went so far as to declare: "If a man died and left sons and daughters and the property was ample, the sons inherit and the daughters receive maintenance; but if the property was small, the daughters receive maintenance and the sons go a-begging." However, later tannaim rejected this ruling on the grounds that the sons could protest: "Must I suffer because I am a male?" Nonetheless, rabbinic sensitivity to the daughter's plight is reflected in the decree that her support from the father's estate be stipulated in every marriage contract. (Jacob Milgrom, *The JPS Torah Commentary*)

Milgrom shows us that though the Rabbis might recognize an inequity in the law, they felt bound not to change it. Instead, they would work around it or compensate for it as best they could. How do you feel about this? Should Conservative Judaism be more flexible when and if a particular law conflicts with our moral sensibilities and/or changed social conditions? Are there times when we must, as our ancestors did, affirm a particular law, even if it offends modern sensibilities?

48. Related through male descent or on the father's side.
49. The Tannaim were the rabbis of the Mishnah — 1st–2nd century C.E.

FINDING A SUCCESSOR

***Moses spoke to the Lord, saying, "Let the Lord, God of the spirits of all flesh, appoint someone over the community who shall go out before them and come in before them, and who shall take them out and bring them in, so that the Lord's community may not be like sheep that have no shepherd."** (Num. 27:15–17)*

A. *Moses spoke to the Lord, saying, "Let the Lord . . . appoint someone over the community"* — This proclaims the praise of the righteous: when they are about to depart from this world, they abandon all thought of their own needs and occupy themselves with the needs of the community. *Who shall go out before them and come in before them* — Not as is the way of the kings of the nations who sit at home and send their armies to battle, but as I have done, I who fought against Sichon and Og. (Rashi)

B. In the Mosaic conception, leadership literally does mean going out in front, as in battle — figuratively, sticking your neck out. No nonsense about the leader bringing up the rear is countenanced . . . Moses' most independent act of leadership is to ask God to set up a new leader. Whatever his fears for the future, Moses has overcome the fear of death and the longing for immortality — the ubiquitous human fear that the world will go to hell without us. Moses teaches his people by leaving them. Were he to go with them to the Promised Land, he would no longer be a leader but a god, always knowing the difference between good and evil, therefore without need of hope or hope for improvement. By being denied their Moses, the Hebrew people were instructed to seek their own salvation anew in each generation. Just as the covenant is constantly broken and mended, so leadership cannot be exercised once or by one for all but only continuously by all together. . . . The major message addressed to Pharaoh has come down to us in story and song as "let my people go!" Only now we know that all along it was intended for Moses. (Aaron Wildavsky, *The Nursing Father: Moses as a Political Leader*)

This is one of the most convincing reasons I know why Moses could not enter the Promised Land. This teaches us about one of the most difficult responsibilities of a leader: finding a successor and letting go. What happens when a leader refuses to let go? How do these ideas play out in government? In volunteer organizations, including synagogues? In family life? What does it tell us about a person's motives to become a leader when he willingly finds and trains a successor?

FOLLOW ME!

***Moses spoke to the Lord, saying, "Let the Lord, God of the spirits of all flesh, appoint someone over the community who shall go out before them and come in before them, and who shall take them out and bring them in, so that the Lord's community may not be like sheep that have no shepherd.** (Num. 27:15–17)*

A. *Who shall go out before them* — Not as is the way of the kings of the nations who sit at home and send their armies to battle, but as I [Moses] have done . . . and as is the way that Joshua followed . . . and so, too, in the case of David, it says (1 Sam. 18:16) *For he went out and came in before them* — went out at their head and came in at their head. (Rashi, based on Sifrei Bemidbar)

B. "Go out . . . and come in before . . . " does not by any means connote merely the leading of troops into battle . . . A man is required "who will go out before them and who will come in before them," one who will "go before" the people as an example for them to emulate in their own lives, both personal and public, "and who will lead them out and who will bring them in," one who, particularly by his own personal example but also by his influence, will be able to bring the people to fulfill all their obligations, both public and personal, in accordance with the dictates of duty. (Samson Raphael Hirsch)

This seems so obvious as to be a truism, except that it is not as common as we would like. Evidently, since Moses chose to stress this point, it was not so common then either! How does this principle play out in the Israeli army, in American Jewish fund raising, and in synagogue leadership? Not long ago, the United States Congress voted to apply the laws they pass to their treatment of their own staffs. What would Moses have said about that?

CUT OUT THE SACRIFICES?

On the sabbath day: two yearling lambs without blemish, together with two-tenths of a measure of choice flour with oil mixed in as a meal offering, and with the proper libation — a burnt offering for every sabbath, in addition to the regular burnt offering and its libation. *(Num. 28:9–10)*

A. Abraham said: Master of the Universe, should Israel sin before You will You do unto them [as You have done] to the generation of the Flood and to the generation of the Dispersion?[50] [God] replied to him: No. He then said to Him: Master of the Universe, Let me know whereby I shall inherit it. [God] answered: *Take Me a heifer of three years old, and a she-goat of three years old* etc.[51] Abraham then continued: Master of the Universe! This holds good while the Temple remains in being, but when the Temple will no longer be what will become of them? [God] replied: I have already long ago provided for them in the Torah the order of sacrifices and whenever they read it I will deem it as if they had offered them before me and I will grant them pardon for all their iniquities. (Talmud Tractate Ta'anit 27b)

B. [In the middle blessing of the Musaf Amidah] There is an introduction, the inverse alphabetical poem *Tikanta Shabbat,* which indicates that God "instituted the Sabbath and desired its sacrifices," and a biblical passage, the command to offer special sacrifices on the Shabbat (Num. 28:9–10). This emphasis on sacrifices may have stemmed from the comment made by Rabbi Yose that one must add some new thought to the Musaf service and that "even if one said, 'And may we offer our obligatory daily sacrifices and the Musaf sacrifice before You,' one has fulfilled the obligation."[52] This section includes a request that the sacrifices be restored — a request that prayer books of the Conservative movement have changed into a historical remembrance of what our ancestors did, rather than a prayer that we be able to offer them

50. The generation dispersed across the earth after the building of the Tower of Babel.
51. The text is related to a general belief that the world is sustained by virtue of the sacrifices, an important part of Israel's holding up their end of the covenant with God founded with Abraham.
52. Jerusalem Talmud Berachot 4:6.

again. The Reform service does not include it at all. (Reuven Hammer, *Entering Jewish Prayer*)

C. In Musaf services (except the alternative for Shabbat), biblical passages describing the sacrifices for the day are preceded by the rubric "some congregations add," indicating that these passages are optional. This follows the view of the twelfth-century rabbi Moses Maimonides (Rambam). In the Musaf service for Festivals these passages, which repeat part of each festival's Torah reading, appear in Hebrew only, with an English summary of their content. *(Siddur Sim Shalom)*[53]

Well, there it is! The Conservative Movement clearly has a problem with the sacrifices. We no longer pray for the restoration of sacrificial worship, and some would skip all references to the sacrifices. The principle enunciated in our first text, that reading about the sacrifices is a substitute for the sacrifices themselves, does not satisfy some, who consider sacrifices a primitive level of religion that we have outgrown. Given that our siddur gives us options, what do you think? Should we read these passages or not? Was it good that our siddur editors eliminated the prayer for the restoration of sacrifices?

TWO WAYS TO UNDERSTAND THE *SHALOSH REGALIM*

A. In striking fashion, the pilgrimage festivals *(Shalosh Regalim)* dramatize Israel's covenant with God and reaffirm our own roles within that partnership. During our *Pesach sedarim,* we assume the status of our liberated ancestors through tales and songs of the Exodus, through ingesting *maror* (bitter herbs) and matzah, symbols of our oppression and divine deliverance. From the second Passover night on, we count down the fifty days of the Omer, anticipating the first morning of *Shavuot* when we will stand for the reading of the Ten Commandments as our ancestors stood with awe and love at Sinai during the moment of Divine Revelation. To spend time in the *sukkah,* a makeshift dwelling with incomplete thatched roof, is to place ourselves directly under God's providential care during *Sukkot,* that same care with which He guarded our Hebrew forebears during their wanderings in the wilderness. We wave the *lulav* and *etrog* in all six cardinal directions indicating that God's commanding, nurturing presence surrounds us wherever we might go. (Rabbi Howard Addison)[54]

B. These three festivals — Pesach, Shavuot, Sukkot — correspond to the three principles that the author of the *Ikkarim*[55] proposed: God's existence, the Divine origin of the Torah, and Divine providence. God's existence and power were confirmed on Pesach by means of the miracles and wonders for [Pharaoh's] magicians acknowledged it, saying, *This is the finger of God.* Furthermore, God's existence was revealed at the Red Sea, so that everyone said, *This is my God and I will glorify Him!* Shavuot corresponds to the giving of the Torah. Sukkot corresponds to God's providence in protecting and defending Israel in the wilderness. (Rabbi Ephraim of Luntshitz)

53. This passage is from the introduction, "On This Siddur," written by the editor of the siddur, Rabbi Jules Harlow. The newer *Siddur Lev Shalem* also has similar alternatives.
54. In *Shutafo: Partners with God — Living and Believing as a Conservative Jew,* published by the United Synagogue of Conservative Judaism.
55. *Sefer Haikkarim* (The Book of Principles), by Rabbi Josef Albo. He considered these three principles to be the fundamentals of Jewish belief.

Rabbi Addison emphasizes two key aspects of the Pilgrimage Festivals: enactment — that they give us ways to dramatize their meaning, and covenant — that they take their significance from the relationship between God and the Jewish people. Why do we need to reenact these occasions in our sacred history? Why isn't it enough just to tell about them or study the concepts? What do we gain from eating matzah and maror, from standing for the Ten Commandments on Shavuot, and from sitting in the Sukkah, that we couldn't get any other way? Rabbi Ephraim gives a theological interpretation of the three Pilgrimage Festivals which fits quite well with the themes of each of the Festivals. Discuss each of these principles: What does it mean to us as Conservative Jews to affirm God's existence, to accept the Divine origin of the Torah, to feel God's providence in our lives? How do these theological ideas function in our lives today? What if we can't believe them as literally as did Rabbi Ephraim?

WHAT CAN SACRIFICES MEAN TO US TODAY?

A. With the exception of the remnant who hope for God's reestablishment of the old Temple worship and prepare themselves for its possible advent in our time, most people would consider the sacrificial cult described in these chapters and elsewhere in the Bible as a "primitive" means of approaching the Creator . . . While a simple dismissal of animal sacrifice as "primitive" may satisfy our sense of modern superiority, it does not give consideration to the underlying purposes of the old practices.

Private sacrifice was meant to place the offerer into a meaningful and direct relationship with God. This was accomplished by bringing the prescribed food to a sacred place, consuming it there in an atmosphere of holy ritual, and at the same time sharing a portion of the sacrifice with the priests . . . It was consumed in an atmosphere of gratitude, exaltation, repentance, or other sentiment appropriate to the occasion for the sacrifice . . . Frequently such cultic meals were the only occasions on which the worshipers would or could afford to eat meat. . . . Public offerings like those prescribed for holy days were to reflect the awareness of the whole community that God dwelt in its midst.

What do moderns consider "primitive" about such rituals? Doubtless, the pre-biblical origins of sacrifice go back to beliefs that the gods desired the food for their consumption. But the Torah itself no longer gives any warrant for the continuation of such beliefs, and Psalm 50:8ff[56] expressly disavows them. Most likely it is the public nature of the ancient slaughtering process that is repellent to current tastes. We prefer to hide behind the walls of abattoirs where the animals are killed in a fashion no less bloody, but without making it necessary for the consumer to witness the life-and-death cycle which goes into his pleasurable nourishment. Moreover, even when we share with others in the eating process, we do not generally experience any of the genuinely worthy emotions which were usually engendered by the sacrifices of old. In the root meaning of the English word, we do not "sacrifice" (i.e., render holy) anything when we eat.

---

56. *I censure you not for your sacrifices, and your burnt-offerings, made to Me daily;*
I claim no bull from your estate, no he-goats from your pens . . .
Were I hungry, I would not tell you, for Mine is the world and all it holds.
Do I eat the flesh of bulls, or drink the blood of he-goats?
Sacrifice a thank-offering to God, and pay your vows to the Most High.
Call upon Me in time of trouble; I will rescue you, and you shall honor Me.

This does not mean that our age ought to be ready for any reconsideration of cultic sacrifice. It does suggest that when seen in its own context the biblical order of animal offerings was a genuine form of worship that cannot be quickly dismissed with prejudicial contemporary judgments. (Gunther Plaut)

Rabbi Plaut addresses the underlying meaning of the sacrifices, which should also remind us that every Jewish table is "Mikdash M'at," a small sanctuary. What can we do to create an "atmosphere of gratitude, exaltation, repentance" when we break bread together, to create an awareness that God dwells in our midst? How often do we eat together as families? With friends? As a community? Why and how does dining together provide possibilities for holiness? What do we lose because of our rushed, fast-food dining habits? What happens to family life when families seldom dine together?

REJOICING ON THE FESTIVALS

A. The Torah does not impose asceticism upon us. It rather desires that we maintain a balance, giving every mental and physical faculty its due, without overburdening one at the expense of another. Prolonged fasting is no act of piety for a weak person whose desires are lessened. Neither is diminution of wealth which has been gained lawfully.

To sum up, our Torah is divided between reverence, love, and joy, through any of which one may approach God. Your contrition on a fast day does not bring you closer to God than your joy on Shabbat and Festivals, if your joy is devoted and wholehearted. *Just as prayer requires thought and devotion, joy in God's mitzvot and God's Torah requires thought and devotion,* for you should rejoice in the mitzvot themselves out of love for the One who gave them, realizing how God has benefitted you. It is as if you were a guest at God's table. Thank God in thought and in word. And if this joy should lead you to melody and dance, this becomes worship and a deep bond of union with the Divine. (*The Kuzari,* Yehudah Halevi)

Reading Halevi reminds us that there have always been people who associate religion with solemnity and a dour demeanor. He asserts that joy is also a part of life, and therefore an essential part of serving God. Thinking about the three Pilgrimage Festivals — Pesach, Shavuot, and Sukkot — what is the joyous element in each? What do they add to our experience of God, Judaism, and Jewish community?

Parshat Mattot

Numbers 30:2–36:13

1. (Num. 30:2–3) Laws concerning vows and oaths.
2. (30:3–17) Vows made by women may be annulled by their husbands or fathers, but only on the day they learn of it.
3. (31:1–51) The war against the Midianites, including the distribution of spoils.
4. (32:1–14) The Reubenites and Gadites ask for the land east of the Jordan.
5. (32:15–32) Moses agrees to their request after Reuben, Gad, and half of the tribe of Menasseh promise to participate in the conquest of Canaan.

THE POWER OF THE PROMISE

If a man makes a vow to the Lord or takes an oath imposing an obligation on himself, he shall not break his pledge; he must carry out all that has crossed his lips. (Num. 30:3)

A. Since people usually make vows or swear oaths when angry, not in a balanced state of mind, the Torah wishes to indicate that the practice of vowing, swearing oaths, etc., is not looked upon kindly. . . . Generally speaking, our Rabbis considered vows frivolous, comparable to the forbidden practice of setting up private altars. The formula in the Torah here is that Moses tells the people to be extremely circumspect if and when they make a vow. There are only two situations when vows or oaths are not frowned upon.

1. If someone feels that in order to cleave to God and overcome his urge to give in to his *yetzer hara* (evil inclination) he needs reinforcements, he may make a vow, forbidding himself something which is basically permitted.
2. When a person forbids himself something which the Torah had already forbidden, in order to reinforce his determination not to transgress such a prohibition.

In either case, the very need to make such a private vow or oath is deplored, but the Torah acknowledges the sincerity of the motivation. The Torah would prefer for such a person not to break his word without the crutch of the formula of an oath or vow. (Rabbi Moshe Alshekh)

To this day it is the custom that when one makes a promise, one says, b'li neder, "without a vow," because Judaism takes formal vows very seriously. However, making a vow can be a support when one is trying to change. In Pirkei Avot, Rabbi Akiva says, "Vows are a fence for abstinence," which means that sometimes one can use them as a discipline. A friend of mine who struggles with his weight once said, "If only I could keep to my diet with the same discipline that I have when it comes to keeping kosher!" In a sense, taking an oath of this kind enables one to say, "For me, this liquor, these cigarettes, these sweets, are tref [not kosher], as if they were forbidden foods." Some questions to think about: Jewish law regarding vows and oaths obviously takes our words very seriously. In these days when people will perjure themselves for pennies, how can we begin to reconstruct the idea that one's word is one's bond? Why is it important to avoid making idle promises? Can the discipline we acquire from observance of mitzvot such as kashrut and Shabbat help us in other aspects of our lives?

ANNULMENT OF VOWS

***If a man makes a vow to the Lord or takes an oath imposing an obligation on himself, he shall not break his pledge; he must carry out all that has crossed his lips.** (Num. 30:3)*

A. R. Yehudah said in the name of Shmuel: Where is the annulment of vows Scripturally intimated, in *He shall not break his pledge*? He may not break it, but others may break [i.e., annul] it for him. (Talmud Ḥagigah 10a)

B. [From the fact that an oath] in substance means that a person commits himself to keep his word and make it true, even as he believes in God's existence, we should infer that an oath should never be able to be voided in any way. However, one of God's acts of lovingkindness toward us — out of God's knowledge of our bodily weaknesses, the limitations of our intelligence, and the constancy with which we change our minds — was to give us a plan by which we could be freed from the constraint of an oath when our wish [in its regard] becomes something new. [We can be released from it] whenever it is possible to make a claim of compulsion or error . . . We are not permitted, however, to go free of it [simply] with an air of disdain, but only through the plan and counsel of a Sage [who can determine that the person sincerely has learned something new that, if he had known of it when he swore the oath, he would not have taken the oath]. . . . He cannot grant himself forgiveness [for the oath], but others can absolve him. *(Sefer Ha-Ḥinukh)*

C. If someone takes an oath or a vow (in Jewish law, a vow involves an object, while an oath pertains to an activity) and then has second thoughts about it, he or she can go to a wise scholar or to three lay people. They can absolve the person on the basis of a declaration that, at the time of making the vow, the person was not fully aware of all its implications.

If, by analogy, we can regard our commitment to recovery as a vow (and oath!), then it surely can be said that there will come times when our commitment will flag — when we will want out. The Torah teaches that we do not have the right to unilaterally violate our vows. We can choose to do so, of course, because we have free will, but it will be at our own spiritual expense.

Before violating our recovery, the program suggests that we call our sponsor or anyone in the program or go to a meeting and talk about it. "Thinking it through" is also a good way to prevent our recovery from being through. Being able to ask for help when you need it is not a weakness — it is a sign of spiritual strength. *(Renewed Each Day)*[57]

One does not have to be an addict or to use the language of recovery to appreciate the wisdom here. Teshuvah, repentance, is also a form of recovery. Sometimes we have to make specific commitments to disciplined change in order to repent. Furthermore, as the Sefer Ha-Ḥinukh puts it, "He cannot grant himself forgiveness [for the oath], but others can absolve him." Why doesn't the law want to trust people's objectivity about their own motives? How does the involvement of other people provide a check on whether or not the vow was made foolishly or hastily? Every year on the High Holy Days we stand up and confess our sins and vow to change. How can we help one another throughout the year in our efforts to live with integrity, to nurture our relationships, to draw closer to God?

DEALING WITH A "SEXIST" PASSAGE

So, too, if, while in her husband's household, she makes a vow or imposes an obligation on herself by oath, and her husband learns of it, yet offers no objection — thus failing to restrain her — all her vows shall stand and all her self-imposed obligations shall stand. But if her husband does annul them on the day he finds out, then nothing that has crossed her lips shall stand, whether vows or self-imposed obligations. Her husband has annulled them, and the Lord will forgive her. *(Num. 30:11–13)*

A. "This is the general principle: Once she has gone forth under her own authority for even one hour, he cannot annul her vow." (Talmud Tractate Nedarim 89a) "[The law of vows] refers to one who is his own master." (Talmud Tractate Nazir 61a)

If vows were made today, would men still have the right to annul women's vows as defined above? That is, is the Torah's command dependent on or independent of the sociological status of women?

Certain laws are true for all time, regardless of social change and the evolution of human consciousness . . . The question confronting us, then, is into which category does male authority over women's vows fall? Is it as immutable as pork chops and adultery or is it subject to reinterpretation as women become independent individuals in control of their own lives?[58] I believe it falls into the latter category . . .

In many cases the Torah states that something is "a statute for all time" *(ḥukkat olam)* or "for

57. "Daily Twelve Step Recovery Meditations Based on the Bible," by Rabbi Kerry Olitzky and Aaron Z.
58. The author gives some examples of earlier practices mandated in the Torah that are no longer done, for example: "women accused of unfaithfulness by jealous husbands no longer drink a potion to prove their innocence, nor does a rapist pay fifty shekels and marry his victim."

all generations" *(l'dorotam)* — for example, the celebrations of Passover (Exod. 12:14), Shavuot (Lev. 23:21), and Sukkot (Lev. 23:412); Sabbath observance (Exod. 31:16); self-affliction on Yom Kippur (Lev. 16:31, 34; 23:31) . . .

Many laws, it is true, are equally binding for all time even though they are stated with no qualifying phrase. The commandments regarding men's annulment of women's vows, however, conclude with a partial qualifying phrase, "These are the statutes *[ḥukim]*" (Num. 30:17). That is, the rest of the phrase, "for all time," is significantly absent.

The general principle that a man cannot annul a woman's vow "once she has gone forth under her own authority for even one hour" could be understood in light of women's modern status as independent persons. Men were given the power to annul women's vows in the past only because a woman was not "in her own control" (Sforno).

Women are no longer dependents who pass from a father's household to a husband's household. Hence we have "gone forth under our own authority" for more than one hour! Because society has moved away from the practice of patrilocal marriage,[59] a married woman today does not generally even move into her husband's household; rather, they set up a new household together or the man might even move into her house (which is not her father's). (Judith Antonelli)

Here we see how a troubling practice in the Torah can be re-interpreted, even by someone who accepts the Torah as divinely revealed (as Antonelli does). The key is the question, "Is the Torah's command dependent on or independent of the sociological status of women?" Asking this question puts one philosophically in the Conservative camp. In terms of our own movement's recent history, the debate about women's roles centered on such questions as, "Is the law regarding women's roles in Judaism innate or sociologically determined by the context of earlier times? Is the changed role of women today merely a passing fad or a permanent change in consciousness?" Do you think that these changes will ultimately affect Orthodoxy, too?

ANGER AND FORGETTING

Moses became angry with the commanders of the army, the officers of thousands and the officers of hundreds, who had come back from the military campaign. (Num. 31:14)

A. The men of the Great Assembly . . . said three things: Be deliberate in judgment, and raise many disciples, and make a hedge about the Torah. *Be deliberate in judgment:* what is that? This teaches that a man should be patient in his speech and not short tempered in his speech, for whoever is short tempered in his speech forgets what he has to say. For thus we find in the case of Moses our teacher: when he was short tempered in his speech he forgot what he was to tell (Israel). . . . For it is said, *Eleazar the priest said to the troops who had taken part in the fighting, "This is the ritual law that the Lord has enjoined upon Moses* (Num. 31:21), (which was to say:) "It is Moses whom the Lord commanded and it is not I whom He commanded." . . . And where

59. The practice whereby a daughter, "who was generally betrothed by her father at a young age, went to live in her father-in-law's household, becoming part of his family, and becoming lost to her own natal family."

do we find of Moses that he was short tempered in his speech? Lo, it says in regard to the officers of the host, *Moses became angry with the commanders of the army* . . . Now is there not an inference to be drawn here? If Moses our teacher, the wisest of the wise, the father of the prophets, forgot what he had to say when he was short tempered in his speech, how much more so we! (Avot D'Rabbi Natan 1)

Jewish tradition considers anger to be a pernicious and destructive force in human relations, best not indulged. Notice here the idea that anger impairs one's intellect, and that the leader/teacher will "lose his teaching" if he loses his temper. A story is told that Rabbi Joseph Soloveitchik was once sitting in judgment, and one of the litigants broke out into cursing. Rabbi Joseph angrily rebuked him — most would say quite properly — but then recused himself on account of his outburst of temper. Was Rabbi Soloveitchik overreacting? Looking around at our society, what negative effects can we see from not controlling anger?

"ARE YOUR BROTHERS TO GO TO WAR WHILE YOU STAY HERE?"

The Reubenites and Gadites owned cattle in very great numbers. Noting that the lands of Jazer and Gilead were a region suitable for cattle, the Gadites and the Reubenites came to Moses, Eleazar the priest, and the chieftains of the community and said . . . "the land that the Lord has conquered for the community of Israel is cattle country, and your servants have cattle. It would be a favor to us," they continued, "if this land were given to your servants as a holding; do not move us across the Jordan." Moses replied to the Gadites and Reubenites, "Are your brothers to go to war while you stay here? Why will you turn the minds of the Israelites from crossing into the land that the Lord has given them?" (Num. 32:1–7)

A. In the case of the Gadites and the Reubenites, you find that they were rich, possessing large numbers of cattle, but they loved their money and settled outside the Land of Israel. Consequently they were the first of all the tribes to go into exile; as is borne out by the text, *And he [King Pul of Assyria] carried them away, namely the Reubenites, and the Gadites, and the half-tribe of Manasseh* (1 Chron. 5:26). What brought it on them? The fact that they separated themselves from their brethren because of their possessions. Whence can we infer this? From what is written in the Torah, namely, *The Reubenites and Gadites owned cattle in very great numbers.* (*Midrash Numbers Rabbah* 22:7)

B. *Then they stepped up to him and said, "We will build here sheepfolds for our flocks and towns for our children"* (Num. 32:16). — They worried more about their property than their sons and daughters, because they mentioned their cattle before their children. Moses said to them, "Not so! Make the essential, essential, and what is secondary, secondary. First build cities for your little ones and afterwards for your flocks." (Rashi)

C. "We, the people of the United States, in order to form a more perfect Union, establish justice, insure domestic tranquility, provide for the common defense, promote the general welfare, and secure the blessings of liberty to ourselves and our posterity do ordain and establish this Constitution for the United States of America."

Reuben and Gad place their individual needs over those of the community, society, and nation. Their focus on the "bottom line" leads them to try to separate from the rest of Israel (to ignore the "general welfare") and to neglect the needs of posterity. Does this sound familiar? If Moses came back today, what would he have to say about our society's priorities, and the behavior of many individuals and corporations?

KEEPING UP APPEARANCES

Moses said to them, "If you do this, if you go to battle as shock-troops, at the instance of the Lord, and every shock-fighter among you crosses the Jordan, at the instance of the Lord, until He has dispossessed His enemies before Him, and the land has been subdued, at the instance of the Lord, and then you return — you shall be clean before the Lord and before Israel; and this land shall be your holding under the Lord. (Num. 32:20–22)

A. When the charity overseers have no poor to whom to distribute [their funds], they must change the copper coins with others, not themselves.[60] The overseers of the soup kitchen,[61] when they have no poor to whom to make a distribution, must sell to others, not to themselves, because it is said, *You shall be clean before the Lord and before Israel . . .*[62] (Talmud Tractate Pesachim 13a)

B. The house of Garmu was expert in preparing the showbread[63] . . . For the following was their memory honored: Never was fine bread to be found in their children's hand, lest people say: These feed from the [preparation of] the showbread — Thus [they endeavored] to fulfill [the command]: *You shall be clean before the Lord and before Israel.* (Talmud Tractate Yoma 38a)

C. *You shall be clean before the Lord and before Israel* — First of all, a person should fulfill "you shall be clean before the Lord" and afterward "before Israel." A person should be meticulous about the *mitzvot* between a person and his Creator, whole-hearted and of pure conscience before the One who knows our innermost thoughts, and in any event he should also be clean in the eyes of other people. For the *mitzvot* between person and person are also *mitzvot* between a person and God, one unified Torah from one Shepherd. This is not the case with one who puts being clean before Israel ahead of being clean before God, for he is not concerned about the honor of his Creator, but does what he does only in order to be clear from other people, which is nothing other than hypocrisy. (Rabbi Meir Simḥah Hacohen)

---

60. Soncino: "Copper coins were unsuitable for keeping a long time, being liable to tarnish and mold. Therefore they would be exchanged for silver ones." Torah Temimah: "[They are not allowed to exchange with their own coins] so that they do not come under suspicion of exchanging them cheaply."
61. The Hebrew word is *tamḥui,* more like a food bank.
62. Steinsaltz: "The implication is that it is not enough to be clean in God's eyes, but you also must be clean in the eyes of Israel [i.e., of other people], that they do not come to suspect you."
63. *You shall take choice flour and bake of it twelve loaves, two-tenths of a measure for each loaf. Place them on the pure table before the Lord in two rows, six to a row. With each row you shall place pure frankincense, which is to be a token offering for the bread, as an offering by fire to the Lord. He shall arrange them before the Lord regularly every sabbath day — it is a commitment for all time on the part of the Israelites. They shall belong to Aaron and his sons, who shall eat them in the sacred precinct; for they are his as most holy things from the Lord's offerings by fire, a due for all time.* (Lev. 25:4–9)

The principle under discussion here is ma·arit ayin, or the appearance of wrongdoing. Clearly, in a position of public trust, even the appearance of wrongdoing is forbidden. This principle also extends to other kinds of behavior. It is the reason, for example, why at some kosher meat banquets you find the parve [non-dairy] margarine still in its wrappers, so that no one, God forbid, would think that it is butter. Rabbi Meir Simḥah presents a contrary view: that it is hypocritical to behave in a certain way only to make the proper impression on others. So what do you think? Do the first two texts hold public figures up to a reasonable or unreasonable standard? Should the rules there, which are essentially about fiduciary responsibility for communal resources, be extended to other situations? Is Rabbi Meir Simḥah's worry about hypocrisy realistic, or is it too purist?

Parshat Mas'ei
Numbers 33:1–36:13

1. (33:1–49) The Israelites' wilderness wanderings, beginning with Rameses in Egypt up to the steppes of Moab across the Jordan from Jericho.
2. (33:50–56) An additional warning to uproot idol worship from Canaan.
3. (34:1–15) Instructions on dividing Canaan among nine and a half tribes.
4. (34:16–29) A list of the tribal heads.
5. (35:1–8) Forty-eight cities are to be given to the Levites.
6. (35:9–34) Laws concerning the cities of refuge, to protect the accidental slayer from the victim's avenging family.
7. (36:1–13) Final discussions concerning the ruling that the daughters of Zelophehad could inherit their father's portion of the Land.

GRATITUDE OR GUILT?

These were the marches of the Israelites who started out from the land of Egypt, troop by troop, in the charge of Moses and Aaron. (Num 33:1)

A. Why the need for this summary? Maimonides explains: "People would think that [the Israelites] sojourned in a desert that was near to cultivated land and in which man can live, like the deserts inhabited at present by the Arabs, or that it consisted of places in which it was possible to till and to reap or to feed on plants that were to be found there, or that there were wells of water in those places. Therefore all these fancies are rebutted and the traditional relation of all these miracles is confirmed through the enumeration of those stations."[64] The midrash testifies to a similar motivation: "The Blessed Holy One said to Moses: 'Write down the stages by which Is-

64. *Guide for the Perplexed 3:50.*

rael journeyed in the wilderness, in order that they shall know what miracles I wrought for them.'"[65] The midrash also records the following view: "The Blessed Holy One said to Moses: 'Recount to them all the places where they provoked Me.'"[66] The ambivalence of the midrash is justified: Scripture attests to both motivations for remembering the wilderness sojourn (e.g., Deut. 8:14–16; 9:7).[67] (Jacob Milgrom, *The JPS Torah Commentary*)

So which is better: to remember God's benevolence or our backsliding? Which is a higher level of spirituality: to serve God out of gratitude or out of guilt? The gratitude is for miracles. Does that speak to us today? Should we feel guilty about something our distant ancestors did?

THE WILDERNESS AND TISHA B'AV

Mattot-Mas'ei always falls during the Three Weeks between the 17th of Tammuz and Tisha B'Av, a time of national mourning for the destruction of both Temples and other tragic events in our history. This midrash relates Tisha B'Av to the desert experience.

A. During all the years that Israel was in the wilderness, on the eve of every ninth of Av, Moses sent a herald throughout the camp to proclaim, "Go out and dig graves, go out and dig graves!" and the people went out and dug graves, in which they spent the night. In the morning, the herald went out and announced, "Let those who are alive separate from the dead!" The living then stood up and found themselves some fifteen thousand short.[68] [And so it continued year after year in this way] until Israel was six hundred thousand short. In the last of the forty years, they did the same thing and, upon finding that they were all still alive, said: Perhaps we have erred in calculating the new moon. So, to make sure [they had the right date], they did the same thing the night of the tenth, each one spending it in the grave he had dug. In the morning, all of them again stood up alive. Then, to make quite sure, they did the same thing the night of the eleventh, twelfth, thirteenth, fourteenth, and fifteenth of the month. Finally, when they saw that not one of them had died, they said: It appears that the Holy One has removed the harsh decree from over us. They declared that day a festival. Accordingly, the sages taught: Israel had no days more festive than the fifteenth of Av[69] and the Day of Atonement. (*Midrash Lamentations Rabbah*, Introduction 33)

---

65. Midrash Numbers Rabbah 33:1.
66. Numbers Rabbah 33:3.
67. Deut. 8:14–17: *Beware lest your heart grow haughty and you forget the Lord your God — who freed you from the land of Egypt, the house of bondage; who led you through the great and terrible wilderness with its seraph serpents and scorpions, a parched land with no water in it, who brought forth water for you from the flinty rock; who fed you in the wilderness with manna, which your fathers had never known, in order to test you by hardships only to benefit you in the end.* Deut. 9:7: *Remember, never forget, how you provoked the Lord your God to anger in the wilderness: from the day that you left the land of Egypt until you reached this place, you have continued defiant toward the Lord.*
68. One-fortieth of the adults died each year. The logic of this midrash, which at first seems quite bizarre, seems to be that in this way they realized that the deaths in the wilderness were not just the normal attrition of mortality, but part of the divine decree that the desert generation would not enter the Holy Land.
69. The Fifteenth of Av, also called Tu B'Av, marked the beginning of the grape harvest. During the second Temple period, it was observed with dancing and singing in the vineyards.

I find this to be a very powerful midrash, in its meditation on human mortality. Perhaps it's the stark way it portrays the winnowing of the desert generation over the forty years. I try to imagine what it would be like lying in that grave, wondering if I would wake up the next morning. Perhaps this midrash still rings true as a parable of human existence: Life and death are no less a lottery now than they were for the desert generation, for all our frantic efforts to prolong our lives. Can this midrash help us confront our own mortality?

OPEN SPACE

Instruct the Israelite people to assign, out of the holdings apportioned to them, towns for the Levites to dwell in; you shall also assign to the Levites open land [migrash] around their towns. The towns shall be theirs to dwell in, and the open land shall be for the cattle they own and all other beasts. The open land that you are to assign to the Levites shall extend a thousand cubits outside the town wall all around. (Num. 35:2–4)

A. *Open land [migrash]* — an open space around the city as an amenity to the city. No building is to be allowed there, no planting of vineyards or any other agricultural activity. (Rashi)

B. The whole domain of a city consisted, therefore, of 1) inner city, 2) common, and 3) fields. Now here it says, "The field of the common land surrounding their cities shall not be sold." The Talmud (*Arakhin* 33b) takes these words in their widest sense: The land is not to be transferred for another use. . . . The field may not converted to a free open space or common; the common not, by being plowed and sown, into a field, or by being built upon, into a city; and equally so, not the city into a field or open space. (*Arakhin*, last Mishnah) "For it is a possession for them for all time." Because it was given to them as their possession for all time, therefore . . . no present moment has the sole claim on it. *All future times have equal claim to it,* and in the same condition that it has been received from the past is it to be handed on to the future. (Rabbi Samson Raphael Hirsch)

Here we have a biblical "greenbelt law." Maimonides extends these rules to all cities in Israel. What is the value of having such open space? According to Hirsch, there is an ethical dimension here. Why does the present moment not have sole claim to this land? Why do we need to have an ethic of how to treat the future? In what ways can we apply both the details of this mitzvah and Hirsch's interpretation of it to our times?

THE ULTIMATE VALUE OF A HUMAN LIFE

The Lord spoke further to Moses: Speak to the Israelite people and say to them: When you cross the Jordan into the land of Canaan, you shall provide yourselves with places to serve you as cities of refuge to which a manslayer who has killed a person unintentionally may flee. The cities shall serve you as a refuge from the avenger, so that the manslayer may not die unless he has stood trial before the assembly. (Num. 35:9–12)

A. Israel's laws of homicide and its system of asylum cities presuppose the following basic modifications in the prevailing practice [of blood-revenge]: 1) Only the guilty party is involved; thus, no other member of his family may be slain. 2) Guilt is determined by the slayer's intention: The involuntary homicide is not put to death. 3) No ransom is acceptable in place of the death of the murderer. 4) The verdict of deliberate or involuntary homicide is made by the state and not by the bereaved kinsman, and to this end asylum cities for the homicide are established. 5) His trial is by a national tribunal and not by the kinsmen of either party. 6) The deliberate homicide is executed by the *go'el* [the nearest kinsman, who had the obligation of revenge under the old system], and the involuntary homicide is banished to the asylum until the death of the High Priest. (Jacob Milgrom, *The JPS Torah Commentary*)

B. If a member of the Jewish people should kill someone, even though it was unintentional, he will feel extremely broken and guilty. He will be so shattered that he has no place in the world to go or to hide. Then God tells him, "I will give you a place. Go to the exile of the refuge city and you will be saved. There you can find peace of mind." But this only applies to someone who has a depth of understanding of what damage he has caused. If a person does not feel this deep regret and still feels he has a place in the world, then the city of refuge is not for him. *(Ḥiddushei Ha-Rim)*

From Rabbi Milgrom, we learn that the institution of the Cities of Refuge was a reform of the practice of family blood-vengeance (still prevalent in some parts of the world), while keeping the focus on the enormity of taking a human life. The City of Refuge was for the unintentional killer, but even that was sufficiently grave to merit some serious consequences. The comment of the Ḥiddushei Ha-Rim is very important here: Only the person who feels regret and remorse for unintentionally causing the death of another person merits refuge. Compare that to today, when so many people show no regard for the consequences of their actions, when people are afraid to express remorse because that might open them up to a lawsuit. What is missing if there is no procedure for the person to work through their remorse and guilt? What do they lose? What does society lose?

THE CAPITAL PUNISHMENT DEBATE: NOTHING MUCH HAS CHANGED

If anyone kills a person, the murderer may be executed only on the evidence of witnesses; the testimony of a single witness against a person shall not suffice for a sentence of death. You may not accept a ransom for the life of a murderer who is guilty of a capital crime; he must be put to death. *(Num. 35:30–31)*

A. Whereas compensation for murder is provided for in all law codes of the ancient Near East, Israel alone maintains that the homicide must pay with his life . . . The concept that there is no commutation of the death penalty for deliberate homicide lies at the foundation of biblical criminal law: human life is invaluable. This idea is not found in any other law corpus of the ancient Near East. (Jacob Milgrom, *The JPS Torah Commentary*)

B. [The rabbis] required that the culprit be warned by two witnesses immediately before the unlawful act carrying the death penalty (after all, he may not know that the act is illegal or punished so severely, and how can you hold him liable for death for transgressing a law that he never knew?); that he respond, "Even so, I am going to do it" (because he may not have heard the warning); that he commit the act within three seconds after hearing the warning (for otherwise he might have forgotten the law that he just heard and therefore could not be held responsible); that the witnesses not be related to each other or to the culprit; and that there be at least one judge on the court who votes to acquit him [for otherwise the court might be prejudiced against him — which, by the way, is the exact opposite of the requirement in American law for a unanimous jury). . . . Put another way, they interpreted the death penalty out of existence, and they intended that result and realized the issues involved fully. (*A Living Tree: The Roots and Growth of Jewish Law,* by Elliot Dorff and Arthur Rosett)

C. A court that has put a person to death once in a seven-year period is called a destructive court. Rabbi Elazar ben Azariah says, "Even once in seventy years." Rabbi Tarfon and Rabbi Akiva say, "Were we members of the court, no person would ever be put to death." Rabban Shimon ben Gamliel retorted, "If so, they would multiply murderers in Israel." (*Mishnah Makkot* 1:10)

D. One who commits murder without witnesses [i.e., with enough testimony to know he is guilty, but short of satisfying every technical requirement of the law] is placed in a cell where he is fed spare bread and scant water [until his stomach shrinks]. Then he is fed barley until his stomach bursts [an indirect method of putting him to death]. (*Mishnah Sanhedrin* 9:5)

Here we see how the capital punishment debate played out in Jewish law. On the one hand, human life is so precious, that no lesser punishment for murder seems adequate. For the same reason, we must be very sparing in applying the death penalty. Yet notice the last source: The Rabbis were concerned lest a guilty murderer escape punishment because of a technicality and threaten society further. Should we require American law to be as careful about certainty of guilt as Jewish law? Is Rabbi Shimon correct in his concern about deterrence? Which is more important, the goal of justice or adherence to the technical requirements of the law?

FLATTERING THE WICKED

You shall not pollute the land in which you live, for blood pollutes the land, and the land can have no expiation for blood that is shed on it, except by the blood of him who shed it. You shall not defile the land in which you live, in which I Myself abide, for I the Lord abide among the Israelite people. (Num. 35:33–34)

A. *Abide* — Hebrew *shokhen* refers to the indwelling of God in his earthly Tabernacle, *mishkan,* from which derives the rabbinic term Shekhinah to represent the earthly Presence of the Deity. The Rabbis state the underlying postulate succinctly: "Because of the crime of bloodshed the Shekhinah departs and the sanctuary is polluted" (Sifrei Numbers 161). The double metaphor of land and sanctuary are two sides of the same coin: The land of Israel is also God's residence and is therefore equivalent in holiness to His Sanctuary. The Lord's demand in the wilderness that the camp be kept pure (see 5:3) is, in Canaan, extended to all of God's land. (Jacob Milgrom, *The JPS Torah Commentary*)

B. *You shall not pollute v'lo taḥanifu* — can also mean, "don't flatter"] — This is a warning to flatterers. *(Sifrei Numbers)*

C. [Explaining the Sifrei] For at first, God warned us against taking a bribe against murderers, and then [here], God warned us against flattering them because of their high position or their power, or the honor of their family, even without taking a bribe, because if we flatter them, we will thereby cause the land to "betray" its inhabitants. (Ramban)

D. Rabbenu Yonah in *Sha'aray Teshuvah* clarified at length the matter of flatterers, and wrote nine sections about them . . . , and the general principle of his words is that one should not flatter a wicked person, and not praise him either to his face or not in his presence, as it says (Proverbs 28:4), *Those who forsake instruction (Torah) praise the wicked, but those who heed instruction fight them.* Included in the principle of flattery is: If he doesn't want to reprove the people of his city, thinking that they will not accept it from him — that is called flattery. (Ḥayyim Vital)

There are two aspects of this offense. The first kind of flattery is not rebuking someone we know is doing wrong. This tacit approval is a form of flattery. The second is worse, because, as Rabbenu Yonah explains, by praising and flattering evil-doers, we confirm them in their behavior; we validate their wrong-doing. Where do we see this happening today? How about the free ride that skilled athletes and other celebrities often are given by the public and the press no matter what their moral character? What about in international relations?

Sources

I made strenuous efforts to attribute everything in this book. The challenge was that I found many of these sources in various collections of comments on the Torah, including Itturei Torah, Min Ha-Torah, Al ha-Torah, and Otzar Ḥayyim. It is the nature of many of these books that they attribute texts but don't tell anything about them (Pliskin has good source explanations at the end of his books). So I had to track down many of these books and authors. I used an amazing four-volume work called Bet Eked Sefarim, by Charles B. Friedberg, which lists and identifies pretty much every Jewish work from 1474–1950. The problem is that in some cases there are many works with the same name, or couldn't be reliably identified either from this reference or internet searches. So some sources are left without identification.

Every darshan has favorite commentaries to use as jumping-off points. I have favored Rashi, the Torah Temimah, and two wonderful books by Zelig Pliskin: Love Your Neighbor and Growth Through Torah, which I strongly recommend. Rabbi Pliskin always seeks out the mussar haskel, the practical ethical application of a verse, and I have learned much from him. I found many of the Mussar texts and stories in his books.

For the English text of the Torah, I used the JPS translation most of the time, though occasionally I followed Everett Fox, Robert Alter, or Richard Elliot Friedman. For the Talmud, I usually used the Soncino Edition or the Schottenstein Talmud. Occasionally I used the translation from the English edition of the Torah Temimah. I consulted the standard translations of Rashi, Ibn Ezra, and Nachmanides, and sometimes used my own rendering of the text.

Abramson, Kassel. (Contemporary, United States) Prominent Conservative rabbi, long served as Rabbi of Beth El Synagogue in Minneapolis, Minnesota; now Rabbi Emeritus. He has been active as a leader of the Conservative movement in the United States.

Abravanel. Don Yitzḥak Abravanel (sometimes pronounced Abarbanel). (1437–1508, Portugal, Spain, and Venice) One of the remarkable figures of the Golden Age in Spain and Portugal — statesman, philosopher, and Bible commentator.

Adar, Zvi. (Contemporary, United States) Samuel and Esther Melton emeritus Professor of Education at the Hebrew University. Dr. Adar writes in the fields of education and Bible study.

Adler, Nathan. (1803–1890, Germany, England) Chief Rabbi of the British Empire.

Addison, Howard. (Contemporary, United States) Congregational rabbi and author, and Gershom Scholem Professor of Jewish Spirituality at the Graduate Theological Foundation.

Akedat Yitzḥak. (1400s, Spain) Torah commentary by Yitzḥak ben Moshe Arama.

Al Ha-Torah. A collection of commentaries on the Torah by Rabbi Mordecai Hacohen (20th century, Israel).

Alshekh, Moshe ben Ḥayyim. (1508–1593, Israel). Often referred to as the Alshekh. He wrote commentaries on the Torah and the Prophets. Although he was part of the important Kabbalistic circle of Safed, his commentary is not Kabbalistic.

Amsel, Nachum. (Contemporary, United States) Rabbi, Jewish educator, and author on Jewish values, including *The Jewish Encyclopedia of Moral and Ethical Issues*.

Angel, Marc. (Contemporary, United States) Rabbi of Congregation Shearith Israel in New York City. He is an exponent of the moderate Sephardic approach to Judaism.

Antonelli, Judith. (Contemporary, United States) Author of *In the Image of God: A Feminist Commentary on the Torah*.

Arugat Ha-bosem. Philosophical work by Rabbi Moshe Ibn Ezra.

Arzei HaLevanon. Book of Responsa by Rabbi Yehudah Leib Tzirelson (1859–1941, Ukraine, perished in the Holocaust).

Arzt, Max. (Contemporary, United States) Congregational rabbi and later Vice-Chancellor of the Jewish Theological Seminary. The quote is from his book on the High Holy Day liturgy, *Justice and Mercy*.

Avnei Etzel. (20th century, Poland) Unfinished work by Rabbi Alexander Zusia Friedman.

Avot d'Rabbi Natan. An aggadic work based on and expanding *Pirkei Avot*, with many passages not found elsewhere in the rabbinic literature.

Azulai, Ḥayyim Yosef David. (1724–1806, Israel, Italy) A leading halakhic and bibliographical authority.

Ba·al Haturim. (1270–1330, Germany, Spain) Nickname of Rabbi Jacob ben Asher. He was a major halakhic authority, whose masterwork was *Arba·ah Turim* ("the four rows"), a comprehensive compliation of Jewish law, whose structure provided the model for the *Shulḥan Arukh*.

Ba·al Shem Tov. (1698–1760, Ukraine) "Master of the Good Name," the name by which Rabbi Yisrael ben Eliezer is commonly known. He was the founder of the Hassidic movement.

Baeck, Leo. (1873–1956, Germany, England) Reform rabbi and scholar, Holocaust survivor, and inspiring leader. He survived Theresienstadt, where he continued to teach and minister to his fellow Jews.

B'khor Shor. (12th century, France) A Talmudist and Bible commentator of the school of Rashi and the Tosafists.

Baḥya Ibn Pekuda. (11th century, Spain) Philosopher and ethicist. He wrote *Ḥovot Ha-L'vavot* ("Duties of the Heart"), an influential work of Jewish ethics.

Baḥ. An abbreviation *Bayit Ḥadash*, a commentary on the Talmud by Rabbi Yeol Sirkus (1561–1640, Poland).

Batzri, Ezra. Contemporary Sephardic Rabbi, authority on Jewish finanacial law.

Be·er Ba-sadeh. Supercommentary to Rashi and Mizraḥi [another supercommentary!] on the Torah, by Meir Benjamin Menachem Danon, chief rabbi of Sarajevo in Bosnia (19th century).

Be·er Hagolah. Commentary on the *Shulḥan Arukh* by Rabbi Moshe Rivkash (1596–1671, Lithuania).

Be·er Heiteiv. One of the standard commentaries on the *Shulḥan Arukh*. The commentary on *Oraḥ Ḥayyim* and *Even ha-Ezer* was written by Rabbi Yehudah ben Shimon Ashkenazi (1730–1770, Germany); on *Ḥoshen Mishpat* and *Yoreh Dei·ah* by Rabbi Zechariah Mendel ben Arieh Leib (1660s–1707, Poland).

Beifuss, Ya·akov. (Contemporary, Israel) Quotations are from *Yalkut Lekaḥ Tov,* his compilation of short essays on the weekly portion.

Beit Sh'muel Aḥaron. (19th century) Collection of Responsa by Rabbi Samuel Fulkenfeld.

Berlin, Rabbi Naftali Tzvi Yehudah. (19th century, Poland) Also known by his initials, the *Netziv*. He was the founder of the great Slobodka Yeshiva and wrote a Torah commentary called *Ha·amek Davar*.

Bokser, Ben Zion. (1907–1984, United States) A leading Conservative rabbi, he served the Forest Hills Jewish Center for almost 50 years and published many scholarly books.

Brooks, Roger. (Contemporary, United States) Formerly Professor of Jewish Studies at Connecticut College, he is now the President and CEO of Facing History and Ourselves.

Buber, Martin. (1878–1965, Germany, Israel) One of the greatest Jewish philosophers of the 20th century. He also translated the Bible into German (with Franz Rosenzweig) and wrote extensively on the Bible.

Bula, Menaḥem. (Contemporary, Israel) Bible scholar, author of the Leviticus Commentary in the *Da·at Mikra* series.

Butzina DiNehora. Ḥassidic work by Rabbi Baruch of Medzibezh (1753–1811, Ukraine), grandson of the Baal Shem Tov. He was an early exponent of Ḥassidic thought.

Cassuto, Umberto. (1883–1951, Italy, Israel) Biblical scholar and historian. He headed both the synagogue and the rabbinical school of Florence and wrote major works on Italian Jewish history, as well as commentaries on Genesis and Exodus.

Childs, Brevard S. (1923–2007, United States) Professor of the Old Testament at Yale University. He was a major Christian Bible scholar.

Cohen, Gerson. (1924–1991, United States) Chancellor of the Jewish Theological Seminary and noted historian.

Da·at Torah. Collection of Mussar teachings by Rabbi Yeruḥam Levovitz (1873–1936).

Da·at Zekeinim. A collection of Torah commentary that originated with the Tosafists (13th century), students of Rashi who also were involved with the creation of the *Tosafot*, commentary to the Talmud.

Darkhei Moshe. Halakhic work by Rabbi Moses Isserles (1510–1572, Poland). Isserles was a great authority on Jewish law who wrote a running commentary to the *Shulḥan Arukh* of R. Yosef Karo.

Degel Maḥaneh Ephraim. A commentary on the weekly Torah portion by Rabbi Ḥayyim Ephraim of Sudlikov (1748–1800, Poland). This work reflects the teachings of his grandfather, the Baal Shem Tov.

Devek Tov. Supercommentary on Rashi's commentary on the Torah by R. Simeon b. Isaac ha-Levi Oshenburk (16th century, Germany).

Divrei Sha·arei Ḥayyim. Commentary on the Torah by Rabbi Ḥayyim Sofer (1821–1886, Hungary).

Divrei Sha·ul. Collection of derashot on the Torah by Rabbi Joseph Saul Nathanson (1810–1875, Galicia).

Dov Baer. (18th century, Ukraine) The Maggid of Mezerich. The disciple and chosen successor of the Baal Shem Tov, the founder of Hassidism.

Domb, Cyril. (Contemporary, England) Professor of Theoretical Physics at King's College, London University. He is a leader of the Association of Orthodox Jewish Scientists.

Dorff, Elliot. (Contemporary, United States) One of the great scholars of the Conservative Movement, with expertise in Jewish law, theology, ethics, and bioethics. He serves as rector and professor of Jewish theology at the American Jewish University.

Dresner, Samuel. (1923–2000, United States). A prominent congregational rabbi, a scholar of Hassidism, and an authority on the teachings of Abraham Joshua Heschel.

Duschinsky, Jacob. (20th century) Hungarian born and trained, Rabbi Duschinsky served as rabbi in South Africa.

Duschinsky, Yerachmiel. (1916–1986, South Africa) The head of South Africa's Orthodox rabbinical court.

Eibeschutz, Jonathan. (1690–1764, Poland, Moravia) Kabbalist and Talmudist, as well as a great orator.

Eiger, Yisrael. (19th century, Pinsk)

Eisenstein, Julius. (1854–1956, Poland, America). Prolific author and communal leader, he was known as *Ba·al ha-Otzarot*, "the master of the anthologies," because so many of his works were collections of sources.

El Am Talmud. English translation and commentary to Tractate Berakhot, edited by Dr. A. Ehrman.

Elazar, Daniel. (1934–1999, United States, Israel) Prominent political scientist. He wrote on both American Federalism and biblical covenant, which he saw as linked.

Elon, Menachem. (1923–2013, Germany, Israel) Renowned authority on Jewish law; served on the faculty of the Hebrew University and on Israel's Supreme Court. His masterwork has been translated into English as *Jewish Law — History, Sources and Principles*.

Emet K'naih. Anonymous work on the subject of truth. Its title comes from Proverbs 23:23: "Buy truth and never sell it."

Ephraim ben Aaron of Luntschitz. (1550–1619, Czechoslovakia) Author of the Torah commentary *K'li Yakar*. He was the Rabbi of Prague from 1604–1619. He also is known as Shlomo Ephraim, the first name added during an illness.

Epstein, Jerome. (Contemporary, United States, Israel) Executive Vice President of the United Synagogue for Conservative Judaism for many years.

Etz Hayim. Edited by Dr. David Lieber, this is the standard Torah commentary of the Conservative Movement.

Eyebescheutz, Yonatan. (1690–1764, Poland, Germany) Talmud prodigy and Kabbalist.

Even Ha-ezel. A commentary on Maimonides' *Mishneh Torah* by Rabbi Isser Zalman Meltzer (1870–1954, Lithuania).

Fackenheim, Emil. (1919–2003, Germany, Canada, and Israel) Major Jewish theologian. He had a particular focus on the possibility of faith after the Holocaust.

Feldman, David. (1929–2014, United States) Conservative Rabbi and renowned expert in Jewish law, particularly bioethics.

Finkel, Natan Tzvi. (1849–1947, Lithuania, Israel) Founder and head of the Slobodka yeshiva. He was a powerful exponent of the Mussar philosophy.

Fishbane, Michael. (Contemporary, United States) Nathan Cummings Distinguished Service Professor of Jewish Studies at the Chicago Divinity School, scholar of Biblical and Rabbinic studies.

Fox, Everett. (Contemporary, United States) Allen M. Glick Professor of Judaic and Biblical Studies and Adjunct Professor of History at Clark University. He wrote a very useful English translation and commentary, *The Five Books of Moses*, which tries to adhere as closely as possible to the Hebrew text.

Frankel, Ellen. (Contemporary, United States) Author and scholar. She is quoted often here from her book, *The Five Books of Miriam: A Woman's*

Commentary on the Torah. In addition to her many writings, she served as Editor-in-Chief and CEO of the Jewish Publication Society.

Fraade, Steven. (Contemporary, United States) Professor of the History of Judaism, Yale University.

Freeman, Gordon. (Contemporary, United States) Rabbi Emeritus of Congregation B'nai Shalom in Walnut Creek, California. He has written extensively on the concept of covenant in Judaism.

Friedman, Alexander Zusia. (1897–1943, Poland, perished in the Holocaust) Orthodox rabbi, leader of Orthodox Jewry in Poland. He wrote a popular commentary on the Torah, *Ma·ayanah shel Torah* (Wellsprings of Torah).

Friedman, Richard Elliot. (Contemporary, United States) Professor of Jewish Studies at the University of Georgia. He is best known for his book, *Who Wrote the Bible?* The citations here are generally from his commentary on the Torah.

Frymer-Kensky, Tikva. (1943–2006, United States) Professor of Hebrew Bible and the History of Judaism in the University of Chicago's Divinity School. Her scholarship had a particular focus on women in the Bible and the ancient Near East.

Garelick, Moshe. (Contemporary, Israel). Author of a weekly column on the Torah portion for the Israeli newspaper *Ma·ariv*.

Gelbard, Sh'muel. (20th century, Israel) Rabbi, author of *Lif'shuto shel Rashi,* a very useful book of explanations of Rashi's commentary, including full citation of the sources Rashi used.

Gillman, Neil. (Contemporary, United States) Professor (retired) of Jewish Philosophy and Theology, Jewish Theological Seminary. He is the author of many books on Jewish thought, including *Traces of God,* an anthology of essays on the weekly Torah portion.

Ginzberg, Louis. (1873–1953, Lithuania, America) Longtime professor of Talmud at the Jewish Theological Seminary. He is best known for his magisterial compilation of Midrash on the Bible, *The Legends of the Jews*.

Goldin, Hyman. (1882–1972, Lithuania, United States) Modern Orthodox rabbi and prolific author.

Gordis, Daniel. (Contemporary, United States, Israel) Rabbi, currently Senior Vice President and the Koret Distinguished Fellow at Shalem College in Jerusalem. He writes frequently about contemporary topics and Israel.

Gordis, Robert. (1908–1992, United States) Major Conservative rabbi and scholar.

Greenberg, Ḥayyim. (1889–1953, Bessarabia, United States) Important American Zionist thinker.

Greenberg, Irving. (Contemporary, United States) Rabbi, founder of the Jewish Life Network (now called The Steinhardt Foundation for Jewish Life). In his long career, he has been a congregational rabbi, college professor, and community leader.

Greenberg, Moshe. (1928–2010, United States and Israel) Major Bible scholar, he taught at the University of Pennsylvania and later at the Hebrew University.

Ha·amek Davar. Torah commentary by Rabbi Naftali Tvi Yehudah Berlin.

Hacohen, Mordecai. (20th century, Israel) Commentator, author of collections *Min Hatorah* and *Al Hatorah.*

Hacohen, Shmuel Avigdor. (20th century, Israel) Son of Mordecai Hacohen. Rabbi of the Masorti congregation in Rehovot, Israel. He wrote a book of essays on the weekly Torah portion called *Likrat Shabbat*.

Ha-d'rash V'ha-iyyun. Torah commentary by Rabbi Aharon Levine.

Ḥafetz Ḥayyim. Rabbi Yisrael Meir Kagan (1839–1933, Poland). Halakhic expert. Also known for his ethical treatises.

Ha-k'tav V'ha-kabbalah. Commentary by Yaakov Tzvi Mecklenburg (1785–1865, Germany).

Ḥakham, Amos. (20th century) Commentator; author of numerous commentaries in the *Da'at Mikra* series published by Mossad Harav Kook. He was also known in Israel because he was the winner of the first Bible Contest in 1958.

Halevi, David. (1586–1667, Poland) Author of the *Turei Zahav* (often referred to by its initials, *TaZ*), one of the most important commentaries on the *Shulḥan Arukh).*

Hammer, Reuven. (Contemporary, United States) Conservative rabbi and scholar. He has served in several leadership capacities for Masorti Judaism in Israel and has written books on midrash, prayer, and the weekly Torah portion.

Ḥanokh of Alexander. (1798–1870, Poland) Ḥassidic rebbe.

Haruzei Penimim. Collection of derashot by Rabbi Yitzḥak Reuven Ornstein (19th century, Poland).

Harvey, Warren Zev. (Contemporary, Israel) Teacher of Medieval Jewish Philosophy at the Hebrew University.

Ḥatam Sofer. Rabbi Moshe Sofer (1762–1839, Germany, Hungary) Legal authority and community leader.

Ḥayyei Adam ("A Person's Life"). A summary of the laws in the *Oraḥ Ḥayyim* section of the *Shulḥan Arukh*, which deals with the daily ritual life of the Jew, along with Shabbat and holy days, by Rabbi Abraham Danzig (1748–1820, Poland).

Herberg, Will. (1901–1977, Belarus, United States) Herberg made a remarkable intellectual journey from Communist activist to Jewish theologian and political conservative. His book, *Judaism and Modern Man*, is still influential.

Ḥiddushei Harim. Halakhic work by Rabbi Yitzhak Meir Rotenberg (1799–1866, Poland). Founder of the Gerer dynasty of Ḥassidism.

Hirsch, Samson Raphael. (1808–1888, Germany) Founder of modern Orthodoxy and author of a massive Torah commentary, among many other works.

Ḥishukei Kesef. Commentary on Genesis and Exodus by Rabbi Moshe Silber (20th century).

Ḥizkuni. Torah commentary by Rabbi Ḥezekiah ben Mano·aḥ (13th century, France).

Hoffman, David Tzvi. (1843–1921, Austro-Hungary, Germany) Rabbi and scholar. He wrote an important commentary on the Torah.

Holtz, Barry. Professor of Jewish Education at The Jewish Theological Seminary, he has published a number of well regarded books on classical Jewish texts and the teaching thereof.

Horowitz, George. 20th century attorney who wrote a useful summary of Jewish civil and criminal law titled *The Spirit of Jewish Law.*

Horowitz, Isaiah. (1555–1630, Prague, Israel) Rabbi and mystic, author of the important work of halakhah, ethics and mystical teaching, *Sh'nei Luḥot Ha-b'rit.*

Horowitz, Pinchas. (1731–1805, Poland, Germany) Rabbi and Talmudist. He is best known for his book *Hafla'ah*, comments on Tractate Ketuvot.

Ḥovot Ha-l'vavot. See Baḥya Ibn Pekuda.

Hurwitz, Yosef. (1848–1919, Lithuania) Student of R. Yisrael Salanter. Rabbi Hurwitz was the head of the Yeshiva in Nevardok.

Ibn Ezra, Abraham. (12th century, Spain) His commentary is noted for its attention to the p'shat, the contextual meaning of the Torah text.

Ibn Ezra, Moshe. (ca. 1055–1108, Spain) Poet, philosopher, and linguist.

Ibn Gabirol. (11th century, Spain) Rabbi, poet, and philosopher.

Igra D'Kallah. Work by Zvi Elimelech, Rabbi of Dinov (1795–1851, Poland).

Imrei Kohen. Work by Rabbi Meir Ha-kohen of Warsaw.

Isaac of Warka. (1779–1848, Poland) Founder of a Ḥassidic dynasty. He wrote a collection of comments on the Torah called *Ohel Yizḥak*.

Israel, Richard. (1929–2000, United States) Author of numerous books. Rabbi Israel was a Hillel Rabbi for most of his career.

Itturei Torah. (1987) Contemporary collection of comments on the Torah, edited by Aaron Ya'akov Greenberg.

Jacob Isaac ben Asher of Pshischa. (1766–1814, Poland) Known as "the Holy Jew." He was renowned for his piety and charity.

Jacob, Benno. (1862–1945, Germany, England) Rabbi and Bible scholar. Author of commentaries on Genesis and Exodus.

Jacobs, Louis. (1920–2006, England) Rabbi and scholar. Founder of Masorti Judaism in England.

Jacobson, Yissachar. (1901–1972, Germany, Israel) Scholar and writer. He published books about the Torah portion, prayer, and the haftarot.

Joseph ben Judah ibn Aknin. (1150–1220, Catalonia, Morocco) Known for his commentary on *Pirkei Avot*, among many other works.

Kafka, Franz. (1883–1924, Prague, Bohemia) Unique modern writer of novels and short stories, including some Biblical parables.

Kehillat Yitzḥak. Collection of comments on the Torah by Rabbi Yitzḥak Reitbard (19th century).

Ketav Sofer. (1815–1871, Hungary) Rabbi Avraham Sh'muel Binyamin Sofer, known after the title of his major halakhic work. The Ketav Sofer also wrote a commentary on the Torah.

Kirschenbaum, Aaron. (Contemporary, Israel) Professor Emeritus and former Chairman of the Department of Jewish Law at the Faculty of Law at Tel Aviv University.

Kitzur Shulḥan Arukh. An abridgment of the major code of Jewish law by Shlomo Ganzfried (19th century, Hungary), translated into English by Hyman Goldin, under the title *Code of Jewish Law*.

Klein, Isaac. (1905–1979, United States) Noted halakhic scholar. He was the rabbi of Congregation Shaarey Zedek in Buffalo, New York, for many years. He wrote the essential book, *A Guide to Jewish Religious Practice*.

K'li Yakar. Torah commentary by Shlomo Ephraim ben Aaron Luntschitz (1550–1619, Prague).

Kol Simḥah. Collection of commentaries on the Bible by R. Simḥa Bunim of Przysucha (1762–1827). Talmudist, merchant, pharmacist, and Ḥassidic rabbi.

Kook, Avraham Isaac. (1865–1935, Latvia, Israel) First Chief Rabbi of Israel, under the British Mandate. He wrote prolifically in the fields of halakhah and Jewish thought.

Korban Aharon. Commentary on the *Sifra* by Aharon ibn Ḥayyim (1545–1632, Morocco, Venice).

Korban ha-Ani. Homiletical commentary on the Torah by Rabbi Jacob Kattina (19th century, Russia).

Kotzker Rebbe — see Menaḥem Mendel of Kotzk.

Kraemer, David. (Contemporary, United States) Librarian and Professor of Talmud and Rabbinics at the Jewish Theological Seminary.

Kushner, Harold. (Contemporary, United States) Best known as the author of *When Bad Things Happen to Good People* and many other books. Rabbi Kushner is currently the Rabbi Laureate of Temple Israel of Natick, Massachusetts.

Lamm, Norman. (Contemporary, United States) Orthodox rabbi and educator. He was president of Yeshiva University.

Leibowitz, Nehama. (1905–1997, Israel) Noted teacher of Torah. Her book, *Studies in the Weekly Sidra*, has nourished generations of students.

Leket Amarim. A collection of talks by Rabbi Yaakov Meir Shechter (Contemporary, Israel). He is a prominent leader and teacher in the Breslov Ḥassidic movement in Israel.

Leon of Modena. (1571–1648, Italy) An unusual character, he is known for his polemics against Christianity and against mysticism.

Levine, Baruch. Professor Emeritus of Bible and Ancient Near Eastern Studies at New York University, author of the *JPS Torah Commentary: Leviticus* commentary.

Levinson, Jon D. (Contemporary, United States) Professor of Jewish Studies, Harvard Divinity School.

Levovitz, Yeruḥam. (1873–1936, Poland) Rabbi and mashgiaḥ ruḥani (spiritual and ethical guide) at the Mir Yeshiva. His masterwork *Da·at Ḥokhmah u'Mussar* is widely studied.

Likutei Yehoshua. (20th century) A collection of comments on the weekly Torah portion by Yehoshua Schenfeld.

Loeb, Mark. (1944–2009, United States) Rabbi of Beth El Congregation in Baltimore, Maryland.

Lubchanski, Rabbi Yisrael Yaakov. (20th century, Poland) Mussar teacher, Rav and mashgiaḥ ruḥani (spiritual and ethical guide) of the Yeshiva in Baranovich, Poland.

Luria, Isaac ben Solomon. (1534–1572, Israel) Known as *Ha-Ari* ("The Lion"). He was a seminal innovator in Kabbalistic thought.

Luzzato, Moshe Ḥayyim. (1707–1747, Italy, Holland, Israel) Best known for his ethical treatise *Mesillat Yesharim* ("Path of the Upright"). Known also as a profound mystic.

Luzzato, Shmuel David. (1800–1865, Italy) Also known by his initials *ShaDaL*. Principal of the Rabbinic College in Padua. A prolific author on many topics, he wrote a Hebrew commentary on the Torah.

Ma·ayanah Shel Torah. See Friedman, Alexander Zusia.

Maharal. (1525–1609, Prague) Initials of Judah Löw ben Bezalel [Moreinu ha-Rav Low]. Great scholar and religious leader. According to legend, he was the creator of the Golem of Prague.

Maharsha. (1555–1631, Poland) Initials of Morenu Harav Shmuel Eliezer Edels. Prominent talmudist. His notes on the Talmud are included in most editions.

Maharzu. One of the standard commentaries on Midrash Rabbah, by Rabbi Zev Wolf Einhorn of Horodna (19th century).

Maimonides. See Rambam.

Malbim. (1809–1879, Romania) Rabbi Meir Leib ben Yeḥiel Michael (Weiser). Author of *HaTorah VeHaMitzvah*, a monumental commentary on the Torah.

Margalit, Reuven. Also Margoliot. (1889–1971, Israel) Prolific author and editor, especially in the field of Kabbalah.

Matt, Hershel. (20th century, United States) Rabbi and scholar. He was a beloved mentor and model to many rabbis.

Maybaum, Ignaz. (1897–1976, Germany, England) Reform rabbi and theologian.

Mei ha-Shiloaḥ. Commentary on the Torah by Rabbi Mordecai Yosef Leiner (1801–1854, Poland).

Meir of Premishlan. (1782–1850, Galicia) Follower of the Baal Shem Tov.

Meir Simḥah Hacohen. Also known as Meir Simḥah of Dvinsk (1843–1926, Lithuania, Latvia). Scholar and halakhic authority with a particular interest in Maimonides.

Meiri, Menaḥem. (1249–1310, Catalonia) Author of a voluminous commentary on the Talmud, as well as a commentary on *Pirkei Avot.*

Mekhilta. Also known as *Mekhilta de-Rabbi Ishmael*, the earliest midrashic work on the Book of Exodus.

Mekhilta de-Rabbi Shimon bar Yoḥai. A lost halakhic comentary on Exodus, known only from quotations in other works.

Mei-imrei Shlomo. Book by Rabbi Shlomo Harkovi, (1890–1943, Russia) Mashgiaḥ ruḥani (spiritual and ethical guide) of the Grodno Yeshiva.

Rabbi Menaḥem Mendel Alter of Kalish. (1877–1942, Poland, perished in the Holocaust) Ḥassidic Rebbe.

Menaḥem Mendel of Kotzk, known as the Kotzker Rebbe. (1787–1859, Poland) Hassidic Rebbe.

Meshekh Ḥokhmah. Torah commentary by Rabbi Meir Simḥah Hacohen (1843–1926, Lithuania, Latvia).

Mikhtav Mei-Eliyahu. The collected writings and talks of Rabbi Eliahu Dessler (1891–1954, England, Israel), one of the outstanding exponents of the Mussar (ethical perfection) movement.

Midrash Avkir. A midrashic work no longer extant, known from being quoted in other midrashim.

Midrash Aggadah. A collection of midrashim on the Torah, consisting mainly of excerpts from the work of Moses ha-Darshan (an 11th-century French rabbi), published by Solomon Buber in 1894.

Midrash Ha-Gadol. ("The Big Midrash") A late (ca. 14th century) midrash on the Torah, compiling earlier Talmudic and midrashic comments and including material not known elsewhere.

Midrash Lekaḥ Tov. Late 11th century midrash on Torah by Tobias ben Eliezer.

Midrash Shocher Tov. Alternate name for *Midrash Tehillim.*

Midrash Talpiot. A dictionary of Midrashic and Kabbalistic concepts by Rabbi Eliahyu HaCohen (1654–1729, Turkey).

Midrash Tanḥuma Ha-Yashan. Literally, "the Ancient Midrash Tanḥuma." *Midrash Tanḥuma* has a complicated and debated textual history, but citation of *Ha-yashan* indicates the belief that the text is from its earliest versions.

Midrash Tanḥuma Buber. An alternate version of *Midrash Tanḥuma* edited by Salomon Buber (1827–1906, Galicia). He was Martin Buber's grandfather and teacher.

Midrash Tehillim. A midrash on the Book of Psalms, known since the 11th century, but whose provenance and dating is uncertain.

Mikra Meforash. Commentaries on the books of the Bible in a modern vein, edited by Abraham Kahana (1874–1946, Israel).

Millgram, Abraham. (1900–1998, United States, Israel) Congregational rabbi, Hillel director, Educational Director of the Commission on Jewish Education of the United Synagogue of America. He wrote a number of books, including *Jewish Worship.*

Mi-Ma·ayanot Hanetzach. Collection of comments on the weekly Torah portion by Rabbi Aharon Surasky (Contemporary, Israel).

Minḥah B'lulah. Commentary on the Torah based on midrashim by Rabbi Menaḥem Porto (1520–1594, Italy).

Min Ha-Torah. Collection of comments on the Torah by R. Mordecai HaCohen, 20th century Israel.

Mirkin, Moshe. (20th century Israel) Edited a widely admired modern Hebrew commentary on the Midrash Rabbah.

Mishnah B'rurah. Commentary to the Shulḥan Arukh by Rabbi Yisrael Meir Kagan (1839–1933), also known as the Ḥafetz Ḥayyim.

Mishneh Torah. Massive code of Jewish law written by Maimonides.

Mivḥar P'ninim. Ethical work attributed to Solomon ibn Gabirol.

M'lekhet Maḥshevet. Philosophic commentary on the Torah by Rabbi Moshe Chaifetz (1663–1711, Italy).

Mordecai Yosef Leiner of Izbitza. (d. 1854, Poland) Hassidic master and founder of a Hassidic dynasty.

Morgenstern, Yisrael of Pilov. (1840–1906, Poland) Grandson of the Kotzker Rebbe.

Moses of Kotzi. See *Sefer Mitzot Gadol.*

Moskowitz, Yeḥiel. (Contemporary, Israel) Author of the commentary on Numbers in the *Da·at Mikra* series.

Muffs, Yochanan. (1932–2009, United States). Professor of Bible and Religion at the Jewish Theological Seminary.

Munk, Elie. (1900–1981, France, United States) Orthodox rabbi and leader. He published a number of important books, including *the World of Prayer* and *the Call of the Torah.*

M'vaser Tzedek. Commentary on the Torah by Rabbi Issachar Dov Ber of Zlotchov, 18th century Hassidic rebbe.

Nachmanides. See Ramban.

Netziv. See Naftali Tzvi Yehudah Berlin.

Nifla·ot Ḥadashot. Commentary on the Torah and the Five Megillot by the Kabbalist Rabbi Samson ben Pesah Ostropoli (17th century, Poland).

Nissenbaum, Rabbi Yitzḥak. (1868–1942, Poland) Prominent Orthodox rabbi and religious Zionist. He was murdered in the Warsaw Ghetto.

Noam Elimelekh. Major work of Rabbi Elimelech Weisblum of Lizhensk (1717–1787, Poland) one of the early rebbes of the Hassidic movement..

Noam M'gadim. A commentary on the siddur written by Joseph ben Meir Teomim (1727–1792, Galicia, Germany).

Odenheimer, Micha. (Contemporary, United States, Israel) Rabbi and activist. He is the founder of Tevel B'tzedek, a social justice organization that is active in Israel and around the world.

Ohel Yehoshua. A work by Rabbi Yehoshua Heller (1814–1880, Lithuania).

Olitzky, Kerry. (Contemporary, United States) Rabbi and author. Currently Executive Director of Big Tent Judaism (formerly known as the Jewish Outreach Institute), he was a pioneer in creating Jewish materials for those involved in the twelve-step process.

Or Ha-Ḥayyim. Commentary on the Torah by Rabbi Ḥayyim ben Moshe Attar, Talmudist and Kabbalist (18th century, Morocco).

Oraḥ L'Ḥayyim. Book of writings on the weekly parashah by Abraham Ḥayyim ben Gedaliah, 19th century Hassidic rabbi.

Oraḥ Meisharim. A work on moral character by Rabbi Menachem Taryash (19th century).

Orkhot Tzaddikim. Anonymous 15th century book of Jewish ethical teaching.

Otzar Dinim U-minhagim. "Treasury of Laws and Customs." A handy one-volume dictionary of Jewish law, edited by Julius Eisenstein (1854–1956, Poland, United States).

Otzar Ḥayyim. Anthology of comments on the Torah edited by Rabbi Ḥayyim Zuckerman (Contemporary, Israel).

Otzar Yisrael. A multi-volume Jewish encyclopedia, written by Julius Eisenstein (1854–1956, Poland, United States).

Owen, Wilfred. (1893–1918, England) One of the great poets of WWI, he fell in battle just one week before the end of the war.

Oznaim La-Torah. Torah commentary by R. Zalman Sorotzkin (1881–1966, Lithuania, Israel)

Pardes Yosef. Torah commentary by Rabbi Yosef Patsanovski (1875–1942, Poland).

Parparot La-Torah. Collection of comments on the Torah by Rabbi Menahem Becker.

Peh Kadosh. Book of teachings by Rabbi Isaac of Volozhin (1780–1849, Lithuania), collected by his students.

Pele Yoetz. This ethical treatise by Rabbi Eliezer Papo (1785–1828, Turkey) has been condensed and translated into English by Rabbi Marc Angel under the title, *The Essential Pele Yoetz: An Encyclopedia of Ethical Jewish Living.*

Peli, Pinchas. (1930–1989, Israel) Rabbi, teacher, author. He was Professor of Jewish Thought and Literature at Ben-Gurion University of the Negev.

Pesukta d'Rav Kahana. Collection of midrashic sermons for holidays and special Sabbaths.

Pinḥas of Koretz. (1726–1791, Ukraine) Early exponent of Hassidism.

Pirkei D'Rabbi Eliezer. A midrashic commentary on the Torah, probably from the Tannaitic period (circa 2nd century CE)

Plaskow, Judith. (Contemporary, United States) Jewish scholar. She wrote a pioneering work of feminist Jewish theology, *Standing Again at Sinai.*

Plaut, Gunther. (1912–2012, Germany, Canada) Rabbi and author. He was the rabbi of Holy Blossom Temple in Toronto for decades and author of *The Torah: A Modern Commentary,* the official Ḥumash of the Reform movement.

Pliskin, Zelig. (Contemporary, United States, Israel) Rabbi and author. He has written many wonderful books emphasizing the moral wisdom of Judaism. He also holds a degree in psychology.

Ra·avad. Rabbi Abraham ben David. (1125–1198, Provence). He is best known for a critical commentary on Maimonides' *Mishneh Torah.*

Rabbeinu Baḥya. Baḥya ben Asher. (1263–1340, Spain) Commentator on the Torah.

Rabbeinu Yonah. (13th century, Catalonia) He is best known for his commentary on *Pirkei Avot* and his ethical work on repentance, *Sha·arei T'shuvah*.

Rabinowicz, Rachel Anne. (1941–1987, United States) Editor of a Haggadah for the Conservative Movement, *Feast of Freedom*.

Rabinowitz, Stanley. (1917–2012, United States) Rabbi of Adas Israel in Washington, D.C., from 1960–1986.

Radak. Rabbi David Kimche. (1157–1236, France) Author of one of the most important Bible commentaries.

Ralbag. Rabbi Levi ben Gershon. (14th century, France) Torah commentator.

Rambam. Rabbi Moshe ben Maimon. (1135–1204, Spain, Egypt) One of the great geniuses of Jewish and human history. He produced a major code, the *Mishneh Torah*, and a great philosophical work, *The Guide for the Perplexed*. He achieved mastery also in the fields of science, medicine, and philosophy.

Ramban. Rabbi Moshe ben Nahman. (1194–1270, Spain, Israel) Rabbi, philosopher, physician, Kabbalist, and biblical commentator.

Rashbam. Rabbi Shmuel ben Meir (1085–1158, France) Torah commentator and legal authority (and Rashi's grandson).

Rashi. Rabbi Shlomo Yitzchaki. (1040–1105, France) Most widely studied of the Torah commentators.

Reishit Ḥokhmah. Highly respected work on morals incorporating Kabbalistic teaching, by R. Eliahu de Vidas (16th century, Israel)

Riemer, Jack. (Contemporary, United States) Rabbi and author. The co-editor of *So That Your Values Live On* and the chair of the National Rabbinic Network, a support system for rabbis across denominational lines. He is a prolific and widely admired writer of sermons, prayers, and books.

Riskin, Shlomo. (Contemporary, United States, Israel) Rabbi and columnist. Formerly rabbi of Lincoln Square Synagogue in New York City, he is now Chief Rabbi of the city of Efrat and writes a weekly column in the *Jerusalem Post*.

Salanter, Israel. (1810–1883, Lithuania) The founder of the Mussar movement, he was a profound moral teacher and exemplar.

Sarna, Nahum. (1923–2005, United States) Bible scholar and Professor of Biblical Studies at Brandeis University.

Sasso, Sandy. (Contemporary, United States) Rabbi and author.

Schorsch, Ismar. (Contemporary, United States) Professor of history, Chancellor of the Jewish Theological Seminary. Among his many writings, Schorsch published a series of online essays on the weekly Torah portion.

Schreiber, Aaron. (Contemporary, United States, Israel) Rabbi and scholar. He is a Professor of Law at Bar-Ilan University Faculty of Law in Israel. Schreiber is the author of *Jewish Law and Decision-Making: A Study Through Time.*

Schweid, Eliezer. (Contemporary, Israel) Professor of Jewish Philosophy at the Hebrew University.

Sefat Emet. Torah commentary by Yehudah Aryeh Leib Alter (1847–1905, Poland). Ḥassidic rebbe and leader of the Gerrer Ḥassidim in Poland. Many of the citations in this book follow the translation of Arthur Green.

Sefer Hafla·ah. Talmud commentary by Rabbi Pinchas Horowitz (1730–1805, Germany).

Sefer Ḥasidim. Pietistic work by Rabbi Yehudah Hechasid (1150–1217, Germany). Rabbi Yehudah was a leader of the movement known as Ḥasidei Ashkenaz, which has nothing to do with the later movement known as Ḥassidism, except that both groups had a mystical bent and emphasized personal piety.

Sefer Ha-Toda·ah. A compilation of the laws and customs for every month of the Jewish year, compiled by Rabbi Eliezer Kitov (20th century, Israel). Published in English under the title, *The Book of Our Heritage.*

Sefer Mitzot Gadol. "The Big Book of Commandments." It is one of the earliest compilations of Jewish law, written by Rabbi Moses of Coucy (13th century, France). It is organized around a list of the 613 Commandments.

Sefer Midrash Aggadah. An anonymous 12th–13th century midrashic collection on the Torah, edited by Solomon Buber.

Segal, Benjamin. (Contemporary, United States, Israel) Conservative rabbi. He made aliyah to Israel many years ago where he has worked on behalf of the Conservative movement in many different capacities.

Sforno, Ovadiah. (1470–1550, Italy). Author of a highly regarded Torah commentary.

Shapira, Rabbi Meir of Lublin. (1887–1933, Poland) Rabbi and educator. He is most renowned for establishing the Daf Yomi program, which coordinates the daily study of a page of Talmud for thousands of Jews all over the world.

Sha·arei Teshuvah. Important ethical treatise by Rabbenu Yonah of Gerona (13th century, Spain). The work not only describes in detail the process and requirements of repentance, but also serves as a guide to Jewish ethics in general.

Shem MiSh'muel. Collection of the teachings on the weekly Torah portion by the Hassidic Rebbe Shmuel Bornsztain (1855–1926, Poland).

Shenhar, Aliza. (Contemporary, Israel) Poet and editor. Chair of the Department of Hebrew Literature and Folklore at Haifa University.

Sherwin, Byron. (1946–2015, United States) Scholar. Long associated with the Spertus Institute in Chicago and respected and renowned in many areas of Jewish studies.

Shmuelevitz, Ḥayyim. (1902–1979, Poland, China, Israel) Teacher. Long associated with the Mir Yeshiva and known for his Mussar discourses.

Sh'nei Luḥot Ha-b'rit. "The Two Tablets of the Commandments." A halakhic work by R. Isaiah Horowitz (1556–1630, Lithuania, Germany).

Shtal, Avraham. (Contemporary, Israel) Writer on Jewish subjects.

Shulḥan Arukh. The major code of Jewish law, compiled in the 16th century by R. Yosef Karo with running notes by Rabbi Moshe Isserles.

Sifrei D'varim. Earliest midrashic commentary on the book of Deuteronomy.

Siftei Cohen. Commentary on the *Shulḥan Arukh*, the major code of Jewish law, by Rabbi Shabtai Kohen (1621–1662, Lithuania, Bohemia).

Siegel, Seymour. (1927–1988, United States) Professor of Ethics and Theology at the Jewish Theological Seminary.

Sigal, Gerald. (Contemporary, United States) Author of *The Jew and the Christian Missionary: A Jewish Response to Missionary Christianity*.

Silber, David. (Contemporary, United States) Rabbi Silber is the founder and dean of Drisha Institute for Jewish Education.

Simḥah Bunam of Pshyscha. (1765–1827, Poland) Ḥassidic rebbe and communal leader.

Soloveichik, Rabbi Yosef Dov Ber. (1820–1892, Lithuania) Known for his great collection of responsa and also wrote a commentary on the Torah.

Sorotzkin, Zalman. (20th century, Poland, Israel) Author of *Oznaim La-Torah*, a commentary on the Torah.

Steinberg, Milton. (1903–1950, United States) Rabbi and author. Served as rabbi of Park Avenue Synagogue in New York City, and wrote many books of lasting influence.

Steinsaltz, Adin. (Contemporary, Israel) Rabbi, scholar, and author. Head of the Israel Institute for Talmudic Publications. One of the most prolific and influential scholars of our time, best known for his commentary on the Talmud.

Stitskin, Leon. (20th century, United States) Professor of Philosophy at Yeshiva University.

Tamari, Meir. (Contemporary, Israel) Economist, teacher, writer. Formerly chief economist of the Bank of Israel, he went onto teach economics at Bar-Ilan University. Tamari has published widely in the field of Jewish business and economic ethics.

Tanna D'Vei Eliyahu. Midrashic work dated to the 10th century. The first part is called *Seder Eliyahu Rabbah*; the second, *Seder Eliyahu Zuta.*

Targum Neofiti. An Aramaic translation of the Torah that was lost and then rediscovered in the 1950s. There is little scholarly agreement as to its dating.

Targum Yonatan. Aramaic translation of the Torah, attributed to Yonatan ben Uzziel (ca. 50 CE).

Teitelbaum, Rabbi Moshe of Uhel. (1759–1841, Hungary), Hassidic rebbe who wrote a commentary on the Torah.

Telushkin, Joseph. (Contemporary, United States) Rabbi and author. He wrote many essential books, including a series on Jewish ethics.

Tiferet Shlomo. Commentary on the Torah and festivals by Rabbi Shlomo Hakohen Rabinowitz of Radomsk, Poland (1803–1866), a Hassidic leader.

Tiferet Yonatan. Torah commentary by Rabbi Yonatan Eyebescheutz.

Tigay, Jeffrey. (Contemporary. United States) Professor and author. Emeritus Professor of Hebrew and Semitic Languages and Literatures at the University of Pennsylvania. He is also the author of the *JPS Torah Commentary* on Deuteronomy.

Toldot Adam. (1774–1856, Hungary and Israel) A book of comments on the Talmud by Rabbi Moshe David Ashkenazi.

Toldot Yaakov Yosef. The first intellectual exposition of Ḥassidism, by Rabbi Yaakov Yosef of Polnoye (1710–1784, Russia).

Torah Temimah. Annotated collection of Talmudic and midrashic comments on the Torah by Rabbi Baruch Epstein (1860–1942, Russia).

Torat Moshe. See Alshekh.

Trunk, R. Yisrael Yehoshua of Kutno. (1820–1893, Poland) Rabbi Trunk was one of the early leaders of religious Zionism and a respected authority on Jewish law.

Tz'ror Ha-mor. Commentary by R. Avraham Seba HaSephardi (15th century, Spain, North Africa).

Tz'vi Elimelech Shapiro of Dinov. (1783–1841, Galicia) Ḥassidic rebbe, founder of the Munkach dynasty. He is best known for his work *B'nei Yissakhar*, a collection of his Shabbat *d'rashot*.

Ungar, Andre. (Contemporary, South Africa, England, United States). Hungarian-born rabbi, doctor of philosophy, liturgist, author, and social activist. He was expelled from South Africa for his anti-apartheid activities.

Urofsky, Melvin I. (Contemporary, United States) Professor of law and public policy and professor emeritus of history at Virginia Commonwealth University. Urofsky wrote a major biography of Louis Brandeis.

Vilna Gaon. Rabbi Elijah ben Solomon Zalman. (1721–1797, Lithuania) One of the greatest scholars of Jewish history, he wrote comments on the Talmud and the Torah, and was a leader of the opposition to Hassidism.

Vital, Ḥayyim. (1543–1620, Israel) Noted Kabbalist, whose work, *Eitz Ḥayyim,* introduced to the larger Jewish world the thought of his teacher Isaac Luria, the seminal Kabbalist.

Warhaftig, Zerach. (1906–2002, Israel). Politician, rabbi, and scholar. He was a founder of the National Religious Party and a signer of Israel's Declaration of Independence. Warhaftig was also an ordained rabbi and a scholar of Jewish law.

Weinfeld, Moshe. (1925–2009, Poland, Israel) Professor of Bible at the Hebrew University. Weinfeld also had a particular interest in Deuteronomy.

Wildavsky, Aaron. (1930–1993, United States) Professor and author. He was a professor of Political Science and the founding dean of the Goldman School of Public Policy at the University of California, Berkeley. He wrote a political analysis of Moses' leadership style titled, *The Nursing Father: Moses as a Political Leader.*

Wolpe, David. (Contemporary, United States) Rabbi and author. He is the Senior Rabbi at Sinai Temple in Los Angeles and a prolific and gifted writer and thinker. Wolpe is also a commentator on the Torah.

Ya·akov of Radzin. (1828–1878, Poland) Hassidic rebbe.

Yehoshualeh of Kutna. (1820–1893, Bohemia) Rabbi and scholar. He wrote a number of works on halakhah.

Yalkut Ha-Derush. A early 20th century collection of sermons in Hebrew edited by Eliezer Lipa Vaisblum and Shlomo Yitzḥak Levitan.

Yalkut Ha-urim. A collection of teachings by Moshe Uri Keller of Tzanz.

Yalkut Lekaḥ Tov. See Beifuss, Ya·akov.

Yalkut Mei-Am Lo·ez. A massive Ladino commentary on the Bible and other works, begun by Rabbi Yaakov Culi, and completed by Rabbi Yitzchak Magriso (18th century).

Yalkut Shimoni. A massive collection of midrashim on the Bible, probably datable to the 13th century. It contains some texts that are unknown elsewhere.

Yalkut Yehudah. Collection of comments on the Torah by Rabbi Yehudah Leib Ginsburg (1888–1946, Russia, United States).

Yavetz, Yosef. (15th century Spain, Italy) He experienced the expulsion from Spain and wrote many works, including a commentary on *Pirkei Avot* which is in print to this day.

Yeḥezkel of Kuzmir. Ḥassidic rebbe (d. 1856) known for his musical gifts and his sermons.

Rabbi Yeḥiel Meir of Gostinin. (1816–1813, Poland) Hassidic rebbe.

Yehudah Ha-Levi. (ca. 1075–1140, Spain) Major Jewish poet and philosopher. His most important work of philosophy is the Kuzari.

Yeruḥam Levovitz. (1873–1936) Influential Mussar teacher at the Mir Yeshivah in pre-war Belarus.

Yitzḥak of Volozhin. (1780–1849, Lithuania) Head of the Volozhin Yeshiva. He took it over after the death of his father, Ḥayyim of Volozhin.

Zalman of Lutk. See Zalman Sorotzkin.

Zeitlin, Hillel. (1871–1942, Poland, perished in the Holocaust) He was a Yiddish and Hebrew writer who was born into the Hassidic world, became secular, and then returned to Orthodox life.

Zev of Strikov. Hassidic rebbe. (1807–1891, Poland) A disciple of the Kotzker Rebbe.

Zipperstein, Edward. (Contemporary, United States) CPA and scholar. A CPA by profession, a Jewish scholar by avocation, Zipperstein published a number of books on Jewish subjects.

Ziv, Simḥah Zissel. (1824–1898, Lithuania) Also known as the Alter of Kelm, he was a student of Rabbi Israel Salanter, the founder of the Mussar movement and became a leading exponent of that philosophy.

Zohar. The most important work of the Kabbalah, Jewish mysticism. Much of it takes the form of a commentary on the Torah.

CPSIA information can be obtained
at www.ICGtesting.com
Printed in the USA
LVHW010359270822
726885LV00011B/233

9 781538 174166